PUCK!

Kirby Puckett:
Baseball's Last Warrior

One of the most enduring images of one of baseball's best loved players: Here Kirby Puckett celebrates his dramatic 11th inning home run that beat the Atlanta Braves in Game 6 of the 1991 World Series.

PUCK!

Kirby Puckett:
Baseball's Last Warrior

Chuck Carlson

ADDAX
PUBLISHING
GROUP

Published by Addax Publishing Group
Copyright © 1997 by Chuck Carlson
Edited by Dan Flannery
Designed by Randy Breeden
Cover Design by Jerry Hirt
Photo Editor Richard Orndorf

ISBN: 1-886110-14-X

Distributed to the trade by Andrews & McMeel
4520 Main Street
Kansas City, MO 64111

Library of Congress Catalog Card Number
3 5 7 9 10 8 6 4 2
Printed in the United States of America

Library of Congress Cataloging-in-Publication Data
Carlson, Chuck, 1957-
    Puck! : Kirby Puckett, baseball's last warrior / by Chuck Carlson
    : foreword by George Brett.
        p. cm.
    ISBN 1-886110-14-X (alk.paper)
    1. Puckett, Kirby. 2. Baseball players–United States–Biography.
    3. Minnesota Twins (Baseball team) I. Title.
    GV865.P83C37 1997
    796.357'092 – dc21
    [B]   97-13818
                                                        CIP

Dedication

To baseball players of all ages, who hopefully have learned something from Kirby Puckett and the unique way he played the game.

Table of Contents

Acknowledgements

This project would not have been possible without the help of the Minnesota Twins organization, especially media relations director Sean Harlin, communications director Dave St. Peter and team photographer Rick Orndorf.

Special and heart-felt thanks, as always, go to the good folks at Addax Publishing including Bob and Sharon Snodgrass, Darcie Kidson, Michelle Washington and the guy who had to deal with this monstrosity most of all, the relentlessly patient Brad Breon.

Thank you, again, to Larry Gallup, my sports editor at *The Post-Crescent* in Appleton, Wis. who gave me the leeway to work on this project. I also owe a debt to *Post-Crescent* news editor Dan Flannery, who came out of the bullpen in the ninth inning and did a great job editing the book.

Also, I'd be remiss if I didn't mention Randy Breeden and Jerry Hirt, who used their special magic to make this book look as good as it does.

Photo by Debbie Sauer

Foreword
by George Brett

There are just certain people in baseball that you feel honored to have played with and against. Kirby Puckett was one of those players. For 12 years, Kirby played the game the way it was meant to be played - with enthusiasm, with class, with all-out energy and, most important, with a smile on his face. For Kirby, baseball was a joy and it made the game fun for everyone around him too.

Kirby Puckett is a throwback to the old school, where you do your job the best you can and you accept nothing less than your best performance. It's a lesson a lot of athletes today could learn.

I remember at the end of the 1992 season, the Royals closed the season in Kansas City against the Minnesota Twins and there was a ceremony honoring me for getting 3,000 hits. I got up to say a few words and as I looked over into the Twins dugout, I saw Kirby Puckett standing there smiling. I waved to him and said, "Kirby, one day this is going to be you, so take notes."

It would have happened too, had he not had a run of bad luck.

But even though he had to retire far before his time, it doesn't take away one bit from what he has accomplished with the Twins and for baseball in general.

But he was more than just a great baseball player (and a sure-fire Hall of Famer, by the way) and a great person, he demonstrated an uncommon sense of loyalty, staying with the same team throughout his career. These days, when a lot of players will change teams depending on where the money is, Kirby stayed loyal to the Twins. It is a rare quality.

Now, Kirby Puckett belongs to history. People can argue all they like about his impact on the game and they can relive his incredible performance in Game Six of the 1991 World Series when he told his teammates to climb aboard and he'd take them to victory - which, of course, he did.

There will never be another like Kirby Puckett. Ever. It was a privilege to play with and against him. He was a special player and a special person and he made baseball something special, too.

Kirby Puckett looks into a sea of media and teammates to announce his retirement from baseball due to the onset of glaucoma. "This is the last time you're going to see Kirby Puckett in a Minnesota Twins uniform." It was an announcement baseball didn't want to hear.

Introduction

Kirby Puckett was the only one who didn't cry.

While all around him grown men and women dissolved into tears, Kirby Puckett faced his future with the same relentless optimism that had fueled everything else he'd ever done.

On this day, July 12, 1996, Puckett wore his familiar Minnesota Twins No. 34 jersey and hat. He joked, he uncorked that trademark cackle when he laughed, he fractured the English language like he'd always done. The only differences were the dark glasses he wore and the white patch over his right eye, the result of the ocular surgery he had undergone just hours before.

And in this jam-packed room in the Metrodome, Puckett, sitting next to his wife Tonya, had come to deliver the news no one wanted but which everyone expected.

"A lot of people understood it was grim," said Dave St. Peter, director of communications for the Twins. "They knew it was bad. But it still sent shock waves through the entire office."

Kirby Puckett, the very definition of the Twins franchise and a goodwill ambassador for a game in desperate need of one, was retiring.

At age 35, and still at the height of his career, the ravages of glaucoma had taken its toll. In an ironic twist, Puckett could see, perhaps better than anyone, that an eye disease had taken away his livelihood.

"For me, a kid from Chicago, coming out of a bad neighborhood, people never thought I would do anything," Puckett said to the packed, emotional room. "And here I am, sitting in front of you guys, and the only sad thing, the only thing I regret that I have about this game at all, is that I know I could have done so much better if I could've played."

Oh, but he did play. Like no other player the Twins had seen before or, likely, will see again.

Bob Costas, the long-time NBC broadcaster and avowed baseball purist, has been a Puckett fan for years. The two are so close, in fact, that Costas' young son is named Keith Michael Kirby Costas.

His first recollections of Puckett came at the end of Puckett's first big-league season, 1984.

The Twins, who had been in the thick of the American League West race, suffered a titanic collapse on the road against Cleveland, blowing a 10-0 lead and losing to the woeful Indians and, as well, letting the division crown slip away to the Kansas City Royals.

"And I remember the next day," Costas said. "It was Cleveland. That old, depressing stadium in a game that meant nothing the day after blowing a 10-0 lead. But I was struck by how upbeat Puckett was. He still had a spring in his step. I thought that was remarkable. He was truly optimistic."

Costas learned that this was no act. He learned that Puckett was indeed that way — in sunshine or rain, good news or bad.

"He's one of those genuinely good people," he said. "And players who are the opposite from him in terms of demeanor — players like Albert Belle and Eddie Murray — are friendly with Puckett. Even if they don't have his same bubbly personality, they respect him for who he is. He gives it everything he has, every minute."

The only player who comes close in that regard, as far as Costas is concerned, was former St. Louis Cardinals great Stan Musial.

"There are just some people who are universally respected and admired," he said. "Even (Chicago Bulls' superstar) Michael Jordan has a few things that edge into the area of controversy and you could contend that makes those people more interesting. But people like Musial and Puckett manage to be true to themselves and offend nobody. That's very rare."

There are, of course, the numbers.

Rare enough is the fact that he spent his entire career with the Twins — and loved it.

He'd had his opportunities to sign big free-agent contracts with other clubs but there was something about Minnesota, the Twins organization and the fans that made any thoughts of leaving fleeting at best.

He was Minnesota's first-round, and third overall, draft pick in

Kirby Puckett, master of improvisation. During the night to honor him on Sept. 7, 1996, the microphone suddenly shut off. Not missing a beat, Puckett used wild hand gestures as he continued to talk into the dead microphone, sending the Metrodome crowd into eruptions of laughter.

1982 out of Illinois' Triton Junior College and made his big-league debut two years later. Naturally, that first game was memorable, as Puckett went four-for-five against the California Angels on May 8, 1984 and became just the ninth player in major-league history to get four hits in his first big-league, nine-inning game.

When his career came to a shattering halt, he was the Twins' all-time leader in hits (2,304), doubles (414), total bases (3,453), at-bats (7,244) and runs (1,071). He was second in triples (57), third in runs batted in (1,085), fifth in home runs (207) and sixth in walks (450).

His 10 All-Star Game appearances puts him third in club history behind only Rod Carew and Harmon Killebrew. He was the Most Valuable Player in the 1993 All-Star Game as well as the only Twin to ever hit .300, get 200 hits, score 100 runs and drive in 100 runs in a season twice in his career.

On top of all that, he was also one of baseball's best centerfielders, winning six Gold Gloves and compiling a .989 fielding percentage.

And, oh by the way, he was also the catalyst for the Twins' two World Series titles in 1987 and 1991. But that's all just cold, hard, raw data.

Where Puckett truly glittered was off the field, in the clubhouse, in the dugout.

Everywhere.

Perhaps because of where he grew up, it was important to Puckett to give something substantial back to the community and he never failed to take the opportunity to do that.

Whether it was working with the U.S. Food and Drug

Administration for stricter food nutrition labels or warning kids about the dangers of tobacco or working with the Make-A-Wish Foundation, Puckett was simply happy to help, glad to give back to the fans and the area that loved him.

These days, he's a force in trying to get a new baseball-only stadium built for the Twins.

To him, that's what it was all about. If you can help, you help.

He has. And he hasn't stopped either. Maybe that's why, even after he'd already retired, Puckett was named as baseball's Man of the Year in October 1996.

"I think Kirby Puckett may be the best ambassador this game has ever had," said Bud Selig, owner of the Milwaukee Brewers and baseball's acting commissioner. "It's amazing. I have never met one person — not one — who has ever had a bad thing to say about him. He exemplifies what baseball is all about. He is what baseball needs."

That's why on his retirement day, there would be no dirges, no sad songs, no tearful good-byes. It would be a celebration of what was, what is and what could be again.

It was an opportunity to thank all those who had helped make his remarkable career possible.

It was a lengthy list. From his family in Chicago, who swore that his dream of playing baseball would stay alive, to his college coaches, to his mentors in the minor leagues who saw something special in this kid, to his major-league teammates.

So many people.

But as often as Puckett was in the right place at the right time, he also made his breaks. He made them with a determination rarely seen these days. He made them because he knew he had to. And he made them because he knew the only thing worse than failing was not trying.

This is Kirby Puckett's story.

A good news story with a happy ending. A story of grit and strength and talent and good humor and fun. And a story that demonstrates that, sometimes, good things do happen to good people.

Perhaps Twins' utility infielder Jeff Reboulet said it best after Puckett's announcement.

"It was an honor to play with him," he said. "I'm just glad to have known him. He was my idol growing up, and he's still my idol."

Join the club.

A mob of fans always seemed to find its way to Kirby Puckett. During a Twins camera day, Puckett was naturally one of the more popular attractions and he took a moment to shake hands with one of his young fans.

CHAPTER ONE
THAT MILLION-DOLLAR SMILE

What does Kirby Puckett mean to Minnesota?

Andy McPhail, the former Twins' general manager, has an idea.

He recalled a time in 1991, shortly after the Twins had won their second World Series and it seemed to sum up perfectly how Puckett and the Twins are inextricably linked.

"After we won the World Series, we had a Twins store in the basement of a glitzy downtown shopping center," McPhail said. "There was a glass door on the front of the store with a big Twins logo.

"There was a long line in front of the store one day, and this little girl — she couldn't have been more than 4 — walked past everyone, went up to the logo, pointed up to it and said, 'Kirby Puckett.' If ever there was a player who was identified more with an organization, and who exemplified more what an organization

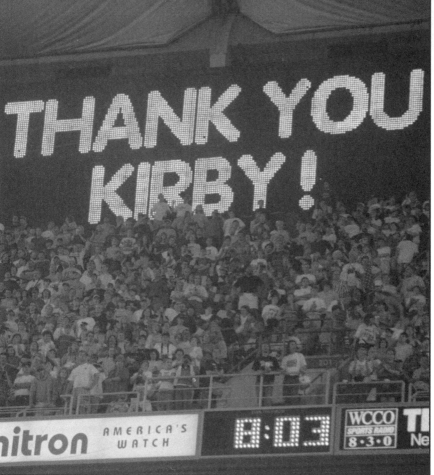

The sign in the Metrodome said all there was to say about what Kirby Puckett meant, and still means, to the Minnesota Twins.

was all about, I don't know who that would be. Kirby was about playing hard and having fun, and that became what the Twins were known for."

That, it seems, will be Puckett's legacy. And a daunting one it is, too.

Even casual observers of baseball know of Puckett and his accomplishments. True, they probably don't know his lifetime batting average or how many triples he hit, but they do know he was a Minnesota Twin, and that counts for a lot.

How many players in today's game can you identify with one team? Cal Ripken with the Baltimore Orioles. Robin Yount and the Milwaukee Brewers. George Brett with the Kansas City Royals. Kirby Puckett and the Minnesota Twins.

There aren't many others. Not anymore. Not in a game in which players bolt from team to team like high-priced pinballs.

Puckett began a Twin and stayed a Twin, not because he had to but because he wanted to. And the people of Minnesota appreciated that. So, not surprisingly, the news of Puckett's premature retirement hit fans hard.

"The game will never be the same," said one fan. "Kirby was the last of the good guys, and there aren't a lot of good guys in the sport."

In fact, mere minutes after Puckett's retirement, sports shops around the state were deluged with requests for Puckett memorabilia.

One store, which had three autographed Puckett baseballs in stock, sold out in less than an hour after his announcement for a cool $100 a piece.

In a pregame ceremony Sept. 7, 1996 to honor Puckett, a car carrying Puckett and his wife Tonya drive below another sign honoring him. It says simply, "You're the greatest, man."

"Phone call after phone call, people are asking if we have anything concerning Kirby Puckett," said another store owner.

Yet another sports shop owner in the Twin Cities noted a marked difference.

"It's not just the kids and it's not just the serious collectors," he said. "We have people who have never bought a card before coming in and buying Puckett's."

And yet another, who sold out of his stock of Puckett items, shook his head in amazement and admiration.

"I love Kirby," he said. "He was the best of the best. It's easy to understand why so many are interested in buying a part of Kirby — they love him also."

Yes, maybe that's it.

There was genuine love for the guy they called "Puck." And it is rare these days to find fans who fall so deeply and completely for a player.

"Not many guys respected the game the way he did," said an Illinois native and Puckett fan.

Respect for the game. Enthusiasm. Love of competition. Loyalty to the team that brought him up through the ranks.

All those things helped contribute to Minnesota's love affair with Puckett.

"What I remember most is how he made watching baseball fun," said Twins' media relations director Sean Harlin. "People remember him for the guy who was a great baseball player and he played it with a smile. When you think of Kirby Puckett, you think of

Photo by Richard Orndorf

Metrodome fans show their love and appreciation for Puckett during his ceremony. Almost from the minute he joined the team in 1984, he became a fan favorite and he never lost it in his 12 years with the Twins.

that big smile, that million-dollar smile of his."

Joe Reis remembers something else.

He remembers going to the memorable sixth game of the 1991 World Series against the Atlanta Braves, the game Puckett nearly won single-handedly with a leaping, home-run saving catch, and later, with his game-winning home run to nearly the same spot.

Reis was in the left-center stands with his wife and two daughters when Puckett's homer sailed into his grasp.

After the game, Reis went to the clubhouse to give Puckett the ball just as Puckett emerged from the locker room and boomed, "What is it going to take to get that ball?" he grinned. "My house?"

You may recall a recent incident with another superstar, Cleveland's Albert Belle, who sought out a fan in Texas who caught one of his home run balls in 1996.

When the fan asked for nothing more than an autograph, Belle cursed him and the fan kept the ball in defiance.

Too often today, that's the image many fans have about pro athletes, especially major-leaguers. They see self-absorbed children who think of nothing but themselves, fans be damned.

But Puckett was different.

Reis offered the ball to Puckett and said, "I hope it ends up in the Hall of Fame with you."

Puckett thanked him, then gave autographs and posed for pictures with the Reis family.

Enough said?

Puckett acknowledges the crowd during the salute to his career.

Yet, that's what endeared Puckett to Twins fans almost from the start.

In fact, by 1988, with barely four seasons in the bigs, he was already a community icon.

A kid from the Chicago projects, he took to the Twin Cities almost immediately and, of course, the community reciprocated.

But it wasn't for his baseball prowess — well, yes, that was part of it too — that the Minneapolis-St. Paul area, the state of Minnesota and baseball in general took to him.

It was because he was so giving of his time. Especially when it came to charity work.

A lot of pro athletes do charity work as part of their contract or because it looks good on TV, but Puckett has always done it because it was the right thing to do.

In 1991, he began the Kirby Puckett Celebrity 8-Ball Invitational pool tournament, drawing athletes and celebrities from various walks. In the seven years it's been held, the tournament has raised nearly $2 million for Children's HeartLink, an organization providing life-saving heart surgery for children.

In 1994, Puckett and his wife Tonya created a scholarship program at the University of Minnesota for students of color.

Over the years, he has also made available 30,000 reserved-seats annually for needy Twin Cities kids who otherwise might not be able to see major league baseball.

Puckett also has a special place in his soul for the Make-A-Wish Foundation, which grants requests for terminally ill children.

Photo by Richard Orndorf

Before long, Puckett's familiar No. 34, a number he really didn't even want when he first came up to the Twins, will be retired by the club.

One 17-year-old Minnesota girl, suffering from bone cancer, asked to meet her hero. Puckett obliged during spring training 1996.

They sat in the dugout and talked about everything and nothing at all. He had his picture taken with the family, signed autographs, gave her some Twins memorabilia and, quite simply, made the life of one sick girl very, very special.

In the clubhouse afterward, Puckett shook his head sadly.

"People always talk about money," he said. "People only see us as baseball players, as money grubbers. This is something. I was almost crying. If I'd stayed out there five more minutes, I'd have been crying. Words can't really express something like that. We're in a position to make a difference in other people's lives. I've always said I wanted to somehow give something back."

For all that work, and more, he won the Branch Rickey Community Service Award in 1994 and was named the Roberto Clemente man of the Year in 1996.

In short, Puckett has done more than run hard on ground outs, come up with timely hits and sign the occasional autograph.

He has given the Twins their soul.

"If I traded Puckett, they'd run me out of town," McPhail said once.

But that was never going to happen. Not in a million years.

Yet there was one point, after the 1992 season when Puckett's contract ran out, when it seemed Minnesota's beloved Puck might leave the Twins for greener, and richer, pastures.

It seemed impossible, but it came close — too close for some fans

Photo by Richard Orndorf

Photo by Richard Orndorf

One of Puckett's favorite off-season events is his charity Eight-Ball pool tournament, which attracts major-league players and celebrities from across the country. Over the years, the tournament has collected millions of dollars for local charities in the Twin Cities.

way of thinking — to happening.

In his 1993 book, "I Love This Game," Puckett acknowledged the possibility of leaving his adopted home.

"I knew I was going to play somewhere in 1993, very possibly with the Twins and at a pretty good salary," he said. "Like (his agent) Ron Shapiro said years before, the worst-case scenario for major league baseball players is still a great case, and we know it."

Puckett filed for free agency after that season and waited for the suits to hammer out a contract that would keep him a Twin for the rest of his career.

But the process went slowly. Too slowly, as far as Puckett was concerned.

The Twins had made an offer to Puckett in November, the same offer team owner Carl Pohlad had said was too high earlier in the process. By this point, Puckett was getting nervous and coming to grips with the possibility that, amazing at it sounded, he would leave the Twins.

At that stage, Shapiro told Puckett and Tonya to think about the unthinkable.

"He asked us to sit down and decide whether we would seriously entertain the idea of going elsewhere, even if we would prefer to stay in Minnesota," Puckett said in his book.

Shapiro's take on the situation was that other teams weren't breaking down Puckett's door for his services because most felt he'd never leave the Twins. So why bother?

If it became clear to the rest of baseball that Puckett would entertain other offers, the dam might just burst.

"Time and energy and credibility were at stake, so Ron wanted me to decide once and for all: Was I prepared to leave the Twins?" Puckett said. "My answer was yes. I was prepared to leave the Twins. You can call it ego or pride if you want; I call it wanting respect."

With all the cards finally on the table, the Boston Red Sox and Philadelphia Phillies dipped their toes in the water and both were offering five-year deals for around $35 million, substantially more than the Twins $27.5 million over the same period.

Other teams showed interest as well, but clearly a line in the sand had been drawn.

Meanwhile, Twins' fans were agonizing over the negotiations and doing whatever they could to keep Puckett right where he was.

He recalled a business trip he made to a downtown Minneapolis skyscraper.

"I was sitting in an office on the 12th floor when I looked out the window and about 20 people were standing on the balcony, holding up a big sign that read, 'Kirby, Please Sign!' I laughed and waved. That was neat."

On November 29, Kirby and Tonya visited Boston, were wined and dined by the front office folks and made to feel as though the franchise would crumble if he didn't sign with them.

The next day, they made the trip to Philadelphia and were impressed with that situation, too.

Now, it was getting interesting. Puckett realized his chances of staying in Minnesota were decreasing by the minute.

"The idea of change had taken hold, especially for Tonya,"

Puckett said. "And the prospect became apparent in Minnesota, too, with suggestions in the media that Puckett could be gone fast and without the Twins having a chance to match any other offer."

It became an excruciating process for Puckett, who was being deluged by phone calls daily from three sides — by friends like Roger Clemens and Frank Viola to sign with Boston; by Phillie friends like Curt Schilling who wanted him there and by teammates in Minnesota who didn't want him to budge.

"I didn't sleep," Puckett recounted in his book. "I'd fall asleep at three o'clock and wake up at six o'clock, thinking about everything."

For Puckett, the struggle had as much to do with loyalty as it did with economics. Yes, the money was good, very good. And he'd be well-paid no matter who he signed with.

But there was another question. Did he want to start over with a new team, in a new situation? Did he owe it to the Twins to stay put? He was an icon in this part of the country and he knew it. If he went to Boston or Philadelphia or somewhere else, would he just be another player?

Yet, the Twins hadn't treated him all that well in the most recent negotiations. Puckett began to wonder if loyalty in this case was a one-way street.

It was simple. Shapiro and Puckett decided that for $28.5 million, Puckett would stay a Twin. But McPhail and Pohlad remained reticent.

"My attitude by then was pretty simple," Puckett said. "A fair offer — very fair, considering the market — was on the table. It wasn't like in Boston or Philadelphia. I knew the Twins organization.

AP/Wide World Photos

One of the most infamous images in Minnesota Twins history is this celebration by Puckett after hitting the game-winning 11th inning home run in Game Six of the 1991 World Series against Atlanta. The next night, the Twins won it all.

They knew me. Did they want to sign me? That's all it came down to."

A tense dinner with Pohlad and McPhail followed, as did another sleepless night in which Kirby and Tonya nearly decided to bag it all and leave the Twins.

But something stopped them. Something intangible. Something more than a huge contract and tons of incentives.

It was, perhaps, a realization that there was nowhere in baseball Puckett could have gone and been happier than he was as a Minnesota Twin.

It wasn't that complicated.

At 3:30 a.m. on Dec. 4, 1993, Shapiro asked Puckett, once and for all, what kind of contract would keep him in Minnesota. Puckett responded with $30 million over five years.

Shapiro relayed the numbers to McPhail, who relayed the numbers to Pohlad.

By 3 p.m. that afternoon, Puckett was at a press conference, telling the media he was a Twin for life.

"Something that nobody really wanted to happen — my leaving the Twins — had almost happened anyway, for a whole bunch of reasons." he said. "But we saved ourselves in the nick of time. In my heart, I didn't want to leave Minnesota, I didn't want to change teams. But only now was the question definitely settled. The day after I signed the new contract, the Twins ran full-page ads in the local papers proclaiming, 'The Puck Stops Here.' That's right."

Consider that entire scenario.

In most instances, players are looking for the slightest reason —
be it money, atmosphere or respect — to leave a team and start
fresh. Puckett was looking for reasons to stay even though he was
given 35 million good ones to move on.

"This is where I belong," he said.

Less than three years later, the Twins made that clear to him on
September 7, 1996, when 51,011 fans — the largest crowd in
more than three years — stuffed themselves into the Metrodome
to honor the man they call Puck.

It was a night to simply revel in what Puckett had done for the
Twins, for the community and for baseball, which badly needed
some shot in the arm.

In the darkness of the Metrodome, Puckett watched on the huge
replay screen as his exploits were relived and relished for all to
see. And though he swore he wouldn't cry, he did. Just a little.
Just enough.

"He looks like you want to hug him and squeeze him and love
him," said one season-ticket holder. "He's just wonderful."

"He's just one of a kind," said another.

The ceremony included Puckett walking from the bleachers in left
to second base, with his path marked by more than 200 youngsters, all of whom Puckett had helped with his charitable work.

During his speech, the microphone went dead, but Puckett kept
the house howling by grandly gesturing as if the crowd could still
hear him.

"I said some pretty funny stuff," Puckett said later, smiling.

But when the microphone came back to life, he said what every Twins fan already knew anyway.

"I think I heard (New York Yankees immortal) Lou Gehrig say he was the luckiest man in the world," Puckett said. "Well, I'm here to tell the Iron Horse (Gehrig's nickname) that tonight, Kirby Puckett is the luckiest man in the world."

More than anything, this was a ceremony for Twins fans — make that Puckett fans. For them, it was a kind of closure, a final realization that No. 34 would no longer be patrolling the outfield or standing in at the plate.

It was a chance for them to tell him how important he was, is and likely always will be.

"Maybe he wasn't born here," said one long-time fan. "But try to convince anyone that Kirby Puckett is not a Minnesotan through and through."

Kirby Puckett's personality was forged at an early age by his parents, Catherine and William, and his eight brothers and sisters. As a result, he never lost sight of how important family is. One of the shining lights in his life, of course, is his little girl Catherine.

CHAPTER TWO
WILLIAM AND CATHERINE'S BABY

 444 South State Street. Apartment 1410.

It began there.

They were the Robert Taylor Homes in south Chicago, barely a mile from Comiskey Park and hard by the non-stop traffic that choked the Dan Ryan Expressway.

This was home to Kirby Puckett, his eight brothers and sisters and his parents, William and Catherine.

They were, and are still for that matter, the projects. And for many who lived there, it signaled an automatic ticket to nowhere.

In Chicago, there weren't many worse places to live than the Robert Taylor Homes, a depressing collection of buildings in which the only thing in abundance was despair.

It's an argument Puckett didn't buy then and doesn't buy even now.

"The standard line they give is that you may very well come out of the Robert Taylor Homes wearing a uniform with a number, but it's more likely to be issued by the state prison, not by a baseball or a basketball or a football team," Puckett wrote in his book. "That reads great. But I resent it. Sure there were gangs when I was growing up at Robert Taylor, and some of the guys I grew up with are dead or in jail. But a lot of good people lived, and still live, in those 'projects' and a lot of good things have come out of those people."

To Puckett, his upbringing in that setting molded and shaped and defined him.

Yes, there were problems and no, this wasn't exactly a Garden of Eden in which to live.

Puckett vividly recalled that when he was 10, a man was stabbed in front of his building and eventually died because no ambulance dared wander into the neighborhood.

There were drugs. There were gangs. There were murders.

But this was also home and, somehow, the problems seemed to bounce off the Puckett clan as if they were surrounded by a force field.

Kirby Puckett was born in 1961, the youngest of nine kids and a full six years after Spencer, the next youngest. The oldest was Charles, 22 years older than Kirby.

The others are sisters June, Frances and Jacqueline and brothers Ronnie and Donnie (twins) and William. By the time Kirby was born, only Spencer and Jackie still lived at home.

"We always had food and clothes and love," Kirby wrote. "I never went without those for a single day in my life."

William Puckett, reputed to be a pretty good left-handed pitcher in the Negro League, worked two 40-hour-a-week jobs to keep the family afloat.

He worked at a department store from early in the morning until noon then would come home for a nap before heading to his job at the post office.

"I would stay up late at night when my dad would come home from his second job," Kirby said. "He'd be home around midnight, when I was still studying, and we'd talk."

So with his father gone so often, the job of raising little Kirby fell to his sisters and to the glue of the family, Kirby's mom, Catherine.

She was a special, driving force in Puckett's life and the person who kept him in baseball, in school and out of trouble.

She was born in Charleston, Mo. and married William when she was only 15.

"She would hang around the cow pasture where the men would play baseball, and that's where they met," said Catherine's only sister, Salitha Smith. "She was a sweetheart darling who was always more concerned about others than herself."

Soon after, they moved to the infamous projects in Chicago, though not because it was the only place they could afford but because it was the only place big enough for the family they knew was coming.

Catherine ruled with a velvet hammer, especially with Kirby.

Photo by Richard Orndorf

Photo by Richard Orndorf

Puckett knew the odds were stacked against him in terms of a major league baseball career. But his mom always told him he could do it and Puckett always knew that if he only got a chance to prove himself, he would convince doubters. He did just that.

"My mom was determined that the baby of the family would stay out of trouble," he said. "I was sheltered, I didn't hang out. I didn't even go to many movies. At night, I was home. It's as simple as that. Baseball and school, that was it, that was my whole life."

He found baseball as a child and loved it from the first. His first bat, in fact, was a rolled-up piece of aluminum foil, his first ball a tightly-wound sock and his baseball diamond was the asphalt canyons of south Chicago.

You make do. You survive. You adjust. It was instilled in Puckett at a young age.

Guiding Puckett was his mom, easily the most important person in his life.

"Kirby was always the closest to mom," Spencer said. "He was kind of a momma's boy."

It was a description Kirby never argued with.

"I guess you could call me a momma's boy, because I was," he said. "She raised nine kids and gave up her whole life for us, and I always said that if I ever made it to the big leagues and made a little money, I wanted her to enjoy it with me."

But back at the projects, that was all just a dream then. So distant. But so close.

It was her influence, along with William's, that forged Kirby Puckett's remarkable personality.

"So many people who come from the same background and environment have some understandable anger or wariness about the world," said NBC broadcaster and Puckett friend Bob Costas. "If he has any of that, it certainly doesn't make its way to the surface.

I imagine his family has a lot to do with that. It may sound trite, but how you react to circumstances is more important than the circumstances themselves."

Puckett never let the circumstances overwhelm him, whether as a kid growing up on Chicago's mean streets or when faced with having to end his baseball career prematurely.

"My personal role models were my mom and dad," he said. "For all nine of us children to grow up and get out of the ghetto and be good, law-abiding citizens, that's a blessing in itself."

It was a blessing as well that Puckett was able to find baseball, and cling to it in circumstances that weren't exactly ideal.

"I played baseball every way I could, every moment I could," Puckett wrote in his book. "I became a master of the sock-ball. Outside, we painted a square on the wall of the building to mark off the strike zone. You could see them all over most of the buildings and almost all the boxes were way too big. In that 'league,' the high fastball always counted as a strike. That's one reason my strike zone was so big."

At the Robert Taylor Homes, the buildings were far enough apart that any fly ball that hit the next building was a home run. If it hit on one bounce, it was a triple and on two bounces, a double.

This was baseball in its purist form. The game made up by kids, for kids. The rules? Heck, you made them up as you went. There were no designated hitters in this game.

Puckett said the rules changed daily, depending on how many kids showed up for a game and there was always one player they could count on being there every day — him.

"When the weather was warm, during the summers, I'd be playing somewhere by eight o'clock in the morning," he said. "And I wouldn't come home until sunset. Even then, I would not come home until I heard my mother's voice calling from the 14th floor. I can still hear her calling today. She was the long arm of the law in our family. Wherever I was, all she had to do was yell, and no matter where I was, her voice would carry."

Puckett spent his first 12 years in the Robert Taylor Homes, then his dad got a promotion at the post office and they were able to move out of the projects and into an integrated neighborhood. By that time, Kirby was the only child still living at home.

Three years later, when he began attending Calumet High, Puckett finally learned what it was like to play an organized game of baseball.

No more home runs off the towering buildings in the projects. No more tearing his pants sliding into the gravel at second base.

At Calumet, he played third base and received the first real coaching of his life from James McGhee. It was an experience he'd take with him the rest of his career.

"We worked real hard on hitting the curveball, concentrating on watching the ball all the way from the pitcher's hand," Kirby recounted. "To achieve the effect of a major league curveball, Coach McGhee cut a slice out of a baseball so it would curve a lot in any kind of breeze."

But while Puckett was clearly McGhee's best player, major-league scouts had yet to find their way to him.

Part of it was that no one really knew about Puckett. Part of it was circumstances.

"They were scared to death to come to our neighborhood,"

Puckett wrote in his book. "And I can't honestly blame them. We didn't even have a real field. No fences. If you hit a line drive in the gap, just keep running."

But even at that stage, as it became clear Puckett had more than just average baseball ability, his family continued to push him.

"My brothers played ball, too, but none got scholarships or anything, so they couldn't pursue the game any further," he said. "They may have been good but they just didn't get the opportunity. They all went to the Army instead. And they helped me by pushing me to be as good as I could be. They urged me to play ball with guys bigger and older than I was, and so I did whenever I had the chance. I'd just squeeze into those games and I was usually good enough to hold my own."

While still in high school, Puckett was invited to play for teams in a summer league with kids far older than he was.

One of those was a semi-pro team called the Chicago Pirates, a team sponsored by a pool hall owner named Roosevelt Askew.

"I played for them whenever I wanted to," Puckett said. "I'd just call and say 'Kew, I want to play today,' and he'd tell me where the game was."

It was just about that time, finally, that the scouts began to notice the little guy with the big game.

He dominated prep all-star games, forcing scouts to take notice even though many were turned off by his size. But Puckett persevered, and for good reason.

"People have always said to me, 'You'll never do this, you'll never do that,' " he said. "I say that all I want from people is just to give me a chance. I can handle it from there. A lot of that confidence must have come from my mother. The rest of my family, too, but mainly my mother. She always said, 'You can do it, Kirby.' And toward the end of my high school years, she started saying, 'You can make it to the major leagues, Kirby.' I believed her. My mom was always positive, positive, positive. I tend to be the same way now."

But despite his perseverance and unyielding belief that he could play baseball at the highest level, he wasn't drafted out of high school.

That was 1979. He was 18 years old and the career he had charted was not fulfilling itself the way he had hoped.

He knew his time was now. He knew he had little margin for error. He knew he needed to convince the people that mattered that he could play this game.

But he never lost confidence and he never lost faith. And neither did his mom.

Even a year later, when Puckett was at Bradley University in Peoria, Ill., and his dad died, there were no doubts about what Kirby would do.

"I went home for three weeks, maybe a month," he said. "My mom was my main concern. I wanted to take care of her. I was the baby, my brothers and sisters were all gone from home, so I figured it was time to step up and show what I was made of."

He even seriously considered dropping out of school to help take care of her. It was an idea she shot down quickly and thunderously.

"You're going back to school," she said. "I've got too many gloves and too many bats and balls invested in you. Plus, you're something special. You're going to make it one day."

In the end, she went back to live by herself in Chicago.

But through the years, the two stayed closer than before, if that was possible.

Catherine watched with pride as her baby moved up the ladder, from college to minor-league baseball to the majors and, eventually, to his first All-Star Game appearance in 1986.

Even when the money began to flow and Puckett tried to show his appreciation to his mother, she would have none of it.

"I wanted to buy her a house because we never had a house before," Puckett said. "But she didn't want a house. 'Too much of a problem.' She didn't want a condo. She didn't want anything."

She wouldn't even accept money.

"If Kirby wanted to give her money, he had to put it on the table and run out," said brother Spencer.

Puckett eventually took to sending her money by Federal Express, with specific instructions that under no circumstances was she not to accept it.

"There was no way she could tell me no," Puckett said.

And though she was proud of his success, she kept it mostly to herself, speaking about her baby only when the subject was brought up by someone else.

"She was proud in her own little way," Puckett said.

But on October 28, 1989, as Kirby was reaching the pinnacle of his career, Catherine died after suffering her fourth heart attack.

She was 65.

"That was the hardest day of my life," said Puckett, who was delayed by a snowstorm and didn't reach her Chicago hospital room until it was too late. "But at least when I had seen her last I was able to tell her that I loved her. Now when I speak to school groups, I tell them that they only have one mom and one dad, so be sure to love them and be sure they know it, because they may not always be with you."

To this day, both William and Catherine remain deep in Puckett's thoughts.

"Mom and Dad were the best people in my life," he said. "They taught me to be responsible and to respect other people's opinions and ideas. That's not always easy to do."

But, as important as his dad was, it was his mom who has shaped him.

"A lot of people are more fortunate than I am," he said. "But I was fortunate to have my mom with me for 29 years. So I can't complain."

Perhaps the most influential person in Kirby Puckett's major league career was Twins manager Tom Kelly. Kelly first saw Puckett as a raw minor league prospect but was impressed with the way he played the game. Eventually, Kelly became the Twins manager and Puckett's career took off.

CHAPTER THREE
A BREAK IN THE ACTION

Knowing you belong and getting the chance to prove it are two very different animals.

And no one knew that better than Kirby Puckett.

He had fallen in love with baseball from the time he was a tot. He learned the game, and developed his skills in the city, not on some lush, green field in a suburban park next to a lake with ducks swimming in it.

He did not hone his skills playing ball in a regimented, baseball-by-the-numbers system. That was not his style. That was not his way.

He learned the game the only way he could, much of the time, by the seat of his pants.

There were no fancy baseball gloves for Puckett, no $200 baseball shoes.

For him, the game was all that mattered. And he played it in sunshine or rain, dark or light, anytime, anywhere, anyhow.

It was an attitude that stood him in good stead because it was the only way he knew how to play, given his circumstances.

Yet even after showing remarkable skills at Calumet High not to mention outplaying guys three and four years older than him in summer league games, Puckett's future looked distinctly limited.

He had graduated from high school without being taken in the major league draft. He knew he'd get only so many opportunities to prove himself before he simply ran out of time and had to get on with the business of living in the real world.

But facts were facts.

So the 18-year-old Puckett, fresh out of high school, decided to take a break from school (never his favorite pastime anyway) and see what the world had to offer. He had received an intriguing scholarship offer to play baseball at a junior college in Miami. But for Puckett, the baby of the family, that was just too far from home.

Instead, he took a job at the Ford Motor Company plant in south Chicago, close to home. Puckett worked on the assembly line, laying carpet in Thunderbirds.

"The pieces of carpet were stacked up beside me, already arranged in the right order to match the color of the Thunderbirds coming down the line," he said. "We had less than a minute to throw a rug in each car and fit it over some bolts sticking out of the floor."

It was fast, tedious work and it paid $9 a hour with a little over-time thrown in. Not surprisingly, though, it was a job Puckett truly enjoyed.

"I don't know what it would be like to toil on the line for 30 years," he said. "But it was a great job for a kid just out of high school."

But, as it turned out, not a lengthy job for a kid just out of high school.

Ford's policy at the time, according to Puckett, was that after 90 days, an employee could become a member of the union.

On his 89th day, Puckett was fired.

"And I know it wasn't because I wasn't doing the job," he said.

From there, he took a temporary job at the Census Bureau just to make ends meet.

Finally, Puckett realized that the time had come to put up or shut up. Either he was big-league timber or he wasn't. He was deter-mined to find out once and for all.

His opportunity came at one of the summer minicamps that sprout up across the country every season. Major-league teams hold tryouts for anyone who thinks they have what it takes to play professional baseball, though most are gravely mistaken.

Nonetheless, scouts show up and look at the talent, just in case there is the diamond in the rough, a player who slipped through the cracks and wasn't drafted.

Puckett took his shot at one of the tryouts, held at Chicago's McKinley Park, just down the street from Comiskey Park and his old stomping grounds at the Robert Taylor Homes.

"What a zoo," Puckett recalled in his book. "Hundreds of guys, it seemed, were milling around at the park, and the scouts and coaches running the show divided us up among six diamonds, ran us through some drills, then set up teams for a game. I played third base, my position at the time, and got some hits."

Puckett's performance caught the eye of Kansas City Royals scout Art Stewart, who pulled Kirby off to the side afterward to talk about his future.

Shortly after that, Dewey Kalmer, the baseball coach at Bradley University, stepped up and introduced himself. Kalmer said he had checked over Puckett's high school transcripts (he was a B student) and was curious if Puckett would be interested in a baseball scholarship.

"I was just shell-shocked," Puckett said. "I didn't know what to say."

He roared home to tell his parents about the stunning change in fortune. They told him to jump at the chance.

As for why he was never a darling of the baseball scouts, he later found out the reason. He was, quite simply, too small.

"My speed they could see and measure," he said. "But they could also see my size. I only weighed about 155 pounds at the time. How were they to know that I would put on so much muscle in the pros? In short, I was not a 'can't-miss' prospect in the eyes of the scouts. I was just a regular prospect, and they're a dime a dozen, literally."

Looking back, Puckett is convinced the year off he took after high school and before the camp may well have worked to his advantage.

"The truth is, I could have a signed a contract right out of high school and never made it past A-ball," he said. "Maybe I needed the year off to grow. Call me a late bloomer."

Whatever it was, Puckett's ship had come in.

He had received a huge break when Kalmer attended the tryout camp. In fact, he was only there thanks to an invitation from Stewart. But Puckett didn't care how or why he was there. He was there and that's all that mattered.

In Puckett, Kalmer saw the usual qualities found in good baseball players: overall speed, decent bat speed and a good arm. But Kalmer also saw overall strength in Puckett and it was a quality Kalmer always placed a lot of stock in.

"He took a chance on Kirby Puckett," Puckett said.

Initially, though, the experience was anything but magical. Told he would play third base (his favorite position at the time), Puckett instead wound up watching from the bench since Bradley started an all senior infield.

"I may have been naive," he said. "But it didn't take me long to figure out that I'd never be playing on a regular basis that season."

But, once again, he decided to make the best of a bad situation.

"The best I could hope for was some work in the late innings," he said. "Mostly pinch-running."

He excelled in that, stealing 10 bases in 10 attempts that first season.

But it was not enough for Puckett, who stormed into Kalmer's office one day and wanted to know just how such a great plan had fallen apart. Kalmer admitted as much and the next day asked Puckett if he could play the outfield.

"I said I could play anywhere he put me," Puckett said. "He hit me some balls and I caught them and there I was — a center fielder."

He had never played the outfield before in his life, at least in any serious capacity. But Puckett knew at the time if he didn't stand up for himself with his coach, his chance would pass.

"I was at Bradley to play baseball," he said. "My mom expected me to play baseball and I was going to do everything I could to play baseball."

By the following spring, Puckett was Bradley's starting center fielder and led the team in home runs and stolen bases while hitting a solid .400. Remarkably, he hit ninth in the order part of the season and still was able to post impressive numbers.

"Didn't have a clue how to get a base on balls, though," he said, developing a trend he would continue through his career with the Twins.

And even though Puckett made the All-Missouri Valley Conference team that season — finally getting serious attention from scouts — he knew his days at Bradley were coming to an end.

The three weeks he'd taken off from school after his father died had hurt his grades and, more importantly, even though he was barely two hours away in Peoria, it was still too far for Puckett from his mom, then living by herself in Chicago.

"There were no bad feelings when I left Bradley," he said. "I sincerely thanked Dewey Kalmer for how he'd helped me. Dewey helped me in particular with my major problem back then: pulling off the ball."

Kalmer did that by putting a tire around his head and resting it on Puckett's right shoulder, thus keeping his left shoulder and arm in sync.

Apparently, it worked.

The following summer Puckett played for Peoria in the highly regarded Central Illinois Collegiate League, a proving ground for years for up and coming baseball talent. What happened next has become a part of Minnesota Twins lore.

It was 1981, the summer that major-league baseball was on strike.

Since much of the Twins organization was shut down because of the work stoppage, Jim Rantz, then a scout for the team, had some time on his hands and decided, along with his wife Pearl, to head south to watch their son Mike play in this league.

In the game, Mike, who played for Quincy, was taking on Peoria, with a short stocky outfielder named Puckett.

Almost immediately, Rantz was captivated by the kid playing center field for the other team. Sure, it helped that he had a great game including a double, a triple, a home run, two stolen bases and he also threw a runner out at home. But there was more to it than that.

"I was not only impressed by his performance on the field," Rantz said. "But it was a very hot day and Kirby was the first player on and off the field. There were 15 to 20 people in the stands after the game — and like Kirby can only do — he came by to say hello to everybody. He hasn't changed a bit."

Rantz didn't talk to Puckett that day but he made a mental note

Photo by Richard Orndorf

Though more known for his offensive skills, Puckett was also one of baseball's top center fielders for years, winning Gold Gloves from 1986-89 and
again in 1991 and '92.

to keep tabs on the kid. Little did Puckett know that day that his life had been changed forever.

Rantz eventually submitted Puckett's name for the Twins to select in the January 1982 draft. The Twins made Puckett their first pick, and the third overall in the draft.

By that point, though, Puckett had already enrolled in Triton Junior College in the Chicago suburb of River Grove and was playing well.

That's when a Twins' representative, Tom Hull, showed up to begin contract negotiations with Puckett.

Puckett, his mom and Hull went to dinner and most of the conversation was handled by Catherine, who only wanted what was fair for her baby.

Then Hull talked terms — a $2,000 signing bonus. Puckett stayed silent no longer.

"I worked at the Ford Motor Company making $2,000 a month," he roared. "Come on now, really."

At that stage, Puckett learned his first lesson about the big, bad world of professional baseball.

Hull made it clear that teams didn't have a lot of money to sign players from the January draft. (In fact, that draft no longer exists because there just aren't that many eligible players.)

Even so, Puckett said he would not sign for $2,000.

Several days later, after speaking with Twins minor league director George Brophy, Hull upped the offer to $6,000, which Puckett again politely, but firmly, rejected.

Puckett knew he was beginning to make a name for himself among scouts and that if he waited until the more prominent June draft, the numbers would be far more lucrative.

"I wasn't worried about passing up six grand," he said.

The dance stopped then and Puckett went on to have a superb season with Triton and he blossomed as a player under the tutelage of coach Bob Symonds.

"Bob was a disciplinarian and he's the most responsible of all my coaches for the way I play today," Puckett wrote in his book. "I learned all the fundamentals from Bob Symonds. He was one of the best baseball coaches I've ever had. And I could talk to him about anything, anytime. He made it clear to each one of us on the team, that not everyone, not even every really talented player, can be a professional baseball player. But he guaranteed that when we left his program, we'd be better people than when we went in, no matter what career we chose. I think he was right."

While scouts shied away from Puckett because of his 5-foot-8, 175-pound frame, Symonds was intrigued by it.

"He had that big chest and shoulders," he said. "Hard as a rock. Always had that big butt, too, and the great wheels (speed)."

At Triton — which Puckett today calls one of the best baseball experiences of his life — he began to develop the character, the personality, the image that would become his hallmark in years to come.

He would joke and kid with teammates, he would be the outgoing guy in the group, the one who kept the team loose when it needed it most.

It was at Triton where he also developed his reputation for shining his shoes.

"I wanted to look professional because scouts were watching," he said. "Plus, I'd always loved shoes and mom told me to take care of the ones I had because we only had so much money. The habit carried over. I'd take my spikes home after the game, wipe the dirt off, polish them up."

Soon, every player on the team followed Puckett's lead.

On the field, Puckett had the kind of season he needed to get scouts to notice. Batting lead-off, he hit .472 for the year, with 120 hits in 69 games, 16 home runs, 81 runs batted in and 48 stolen bases. For his performance, he was named the Junior College player of the year for that region.

Triton went to the Junior College World Series in Grand Junction, Colo., and Puckett set the place on fire.

Symonds recalled Triton's first game of the tournament.

"Kirby hit the first pitch of the game into the gap and flew around the bases for a triple," he said. "The crowd went wild watching him leg out the triple. They spent the rest of the week coming out to cheer for Kirby."

Triton finished fifth overall and Puckett went 11 for 16 with four triples and four doubles.

"I was on the top of my game back then," he said.

Years later, Triton retired Puckett's No. 29, though he only spent one season at the school.

That June, the Twins, who still owned Puckett's draft rights from

January, were back. And this time, no one was talking about $6,000 signing bonuses.

"All of a sudden — in about 18 months — I'd gone from being a regular prospect at best to something of a hot property," Puckett said.

Several teams told Puckett and his mom that if they waited for the next draft later that month, he could sign for $100,000, but Puckett knew better.

This time, the Twins sent Ellsworth Brown to negotiate (Tom Hull had died of a heart attack a few months earlier while shoveling snow). Brown had kept a close eye on Puckett, watching several of his games at Triton and observing as he blossomed as an all-around player.

Puckett knew he held most of the cards as it concerned the Twins, but he also had a pretty decent grasp on the practical.

At the time, Calvin Griffith still owned the Twins. Puckett had heard, rightly or wrongly, that Griffith was interested in dumping high-salaried players for younger, hungrier, cheaper players.

Puckett fit right into that mold.

"That was fine with me because it meant I'd have a chance to move up fast," he said. "That's all I wanted. I was on a mission to make the big leagues. I wanted a good (signing) bonus, but even more I liked the idea of moving up fast with the Twins."

As arduous as the January negotiation had been with Hull, that's how simple the June talk with Brown was.

In Puckett's hotel room, Brown offered a $20,000 bonus and Puckett accepted on the spot.

"So my 'holdout' six months before had already made me $14,000," Puckett said. "That tickled me."

With his new-found wealth, Puckett gave half to his mom and eventually bought a used 1980 Buick Skylark. "It was the most valuable thing I'd ever owned," he said.

Shortly after that, Puckett was assigned to the Twins Appalachian League team in Elizabethton, Tenn., a town of 12,000 souls in the hills of the southern Tennessee.

It was just rookie ball, but it didn't matter because the journey was under way.

Puckett, by virtue of his "advanced" age of 21 and his "fortune" of $20,000, automatically became a leader of a team that mostly featured 18 and 19 year-old kids signed out of high school.

"Puck always had a gang," said Charlie Manuel, the Twins' roving minor league hitting coach in the early 1980s. "He always had a bunch of guys around him. He was a natural leader by example. He was electrifying."

But that didn't mean the Twins still didn't have some questions about their top draft pick. As a result, he was moved from center field, a position he was growing truly comfortable playing, to left field — ostensibly because his arm wasn't strong enough.

The move amused Puckett at first because he knew, eventually, the Twins would realize their error and move him back where he belonged.

He was right.

Puckett's first pro season was no different than from what a thousand other prospective players have gone through in a thousand other towns in a thousand other circumstances.

He shared an insect-infested apartment with two other players and when the team returned from road trips, the place was barely inhabitable because of the roaches.

But such is life in the bushes. And Puckett knew it.

Besides, with the way he was performing on the field, he knew Elizabethton, Tenn. would soon be in his rear-view mirror.

In fact, whenever Manuel was in town, Puckett would make a point of searching him out and grilling him.

"How do I get to the big leagues?" he'd ask Manuel.

"By getting hits," Manuel replied.

"I can do that," countered Puckett with a smile.

Manuel recalled a time when Puckett came up to him with a serious question.

"He said, 'Charlie, don't you like black players? You never work with me on my hitting,' " Manuel said. "And I told him, 'You can hit. I don't want to work with you. I'll just mess you up.' And I meant that."

Puckett proved it, too.

In 65 games at Elizabethton, Puckett scorched the league, hitting .382 with 105 hits, 135 total bases and 43 stolen bases — all of which led the league. He also led the league's outfielders in assists, putouts and total chances.

Manuel met Puckett for the first time that year when the team was passing out uniforms.

"He got on his uniform and we went out to the field to practice, and I remember seeing him run and throw the ball," he said. "He was grinning and having fun like he had been there before. He stood out like a sore thumb, the way he hustled, the way he played, the way he smiled. And the biggest thing was the way he could hit the ball."

Early in the season, Elizabethton's manager, Freddy Waters, asked his staff, including Manuel, if they saw any potential big leaguers on the team. Manuel immediately chimed in with Puckett's name. Waters smiled and simply nodded.

After conquering rookie ball, Puckett went to Florida that fall to participate in his first Instructional League, where he met the most influential baseball people of his life — coaches Tom Kelly, Cal Ermer and Rick Stelmaszek.

Initially, Puckett struggled in Florida but when Kelly, who was coaching Puckett's team, asked Stelmaszek which players he was interested in seeing, the intrigued Stelmaszek mentioned Puckett.

"OK," Kelly said. "But he hasn't done much so far."

It didn't matter to Stelmaszek.

"Well, I'd like to see him anyway," he said.

As Puckett recounts, it made all the difference in the world.

"And starting on that day, I was on fire," he said. "I played really well most of that six-week camp, which was good timing because that was the first time most of the Twins' upper echelon had seen me play."

Of course, there may have been another reason why Puckett began playing well — a "Kirby" tattoo he had put on his left bicep.

"And I started hitting the ball hard," he said.

It was the best $8 he ever spent.

For the past 18 months, Puckett had been clearing hurdle after hurdle on his inexorable trip to the major leagues.

First he got his break at the major-league tryout camp when Bradley's Dewey Kalmer found him. Then came his summer in the Central Illinois Collegiate League, when Twins' scout Jim Rantz just happened to see him. Then came his formative stop at Triton Junior College when he became more than a decent prospect and evolved into a serious baseball player.

What followed was a superb stint first with the Twins' rookie league team in Tennessee then a solid Instructional League where the people who mattered were finally paying attention.

In 1983, the decision was whether to send Puckett to the Twins' "low" Class A team in Kenosha, Wis. or to their "high" Class A squad in Visalia, Calif. Actually, there was no decision to be made — that season Puckett was in Visalia.

Once again, Puckett thrived. He began the year with a 16-game hitting streak and he never really slowed down.

Despite playing most of the season with aching hamstrings, he hit .314 with nine home runs and 97 runs batted in and stole 48 bases. In the outfield, he made just three errors and threw out 24 runners. For all of that, he was named California League player of the year.

Continuing his remarkable progress, Puckett went back to Instructional League that fall and hit a solid .350.

Not surprisingly, the numbers Puckett posted that season were the best of any prospect in the Twins' organization and Puckett felt, when camp opened in 1984, he'd be invited to the big-league camp in Orlando, Fla., instead of the minor-league camp in Melbourne.

It didn't work that way.

Minor league director George Brophy, bound by the complicated roster rules, had several other players he needed to protect on the team's major league 40-man roster. Since Puckett had less than three years of pro experience, he was in no danger of being stolen by another team. As a result, he could stay in the minor-league camp while the Twins looked at several other prospects.

Puckett understood just enough of the process and he knew it made sense. That didn't mean he liked it.

"I didn't figure that I'd be going to the big club in 1984," he said. "I just wanted to go to the big league spring training camp to meet all those guys. I was in awe of them, and I wanted to be one of them, if only for six weeks. I thought that was a privilege I had earned with my play. In any other organization, I would've been invited to the big league camp. I know that. I understand the Twins thinking now, but at the time I was really upset."

He was especially upset when he learned who the Twins had invited to the big league camp and none of them exactly ended up on the fast track to the Hall of Fame.

"My reaction that spring just goes to show why so many young baseball players are so insecure," Puckett said. "Your future in the game, no matter how well you play, is in somebody else's hands until you make the majors. And then it still is, most of the time."

But spurred by the snub, Puckett rededicated himself to making the most of the 1984 season — wherever he ended up.

And there was some serious lobbying going on for Puckett's services that season between Charlie Manuel at Class AA Orlando and Cal Ermer, who wanted him for the AAA club in Toledo, Ohio.

Manuel went as far as to try and hide Puckett during split-squad spring games, sending him to the game he knew no one would watch. He'd also jokingly offer Puckett the keys to his prized '65 Mustang to take for a spin during games.

But it didn't work. By the end of spring training, Puckett was on his way to being a Toledo Mud Hen.

For the better part of two years, Puckett had his way with pro baseball. But now, it was getting serious as he made the move to Class AAA, a rung below the big time.

"I do know that the jump from Class A to Triple A is a big one," he said. "I roped about 15 line drives in my first 15 at-bats during the season."

Then Puckett was introduced to something he'd never seen before — quality, killer sliders.

"I saw a lot of good sliders for the first time," he said. "And no more fastballs right down the chute on 3-0, 3-1. I'd always been a free swinger with a tendency to help out the pitcher by going after some bad pitches, and nothing's tougher to hit than a hard slider a foot off the plate. Man, it's going to be tough from now on, I thought."

Indeed, it took a few weeks to get his bearings and learn how to hit better pitching. But, as he'd always done, he adapted and thrived.

Barely a month into Toledo's season, Puckett was hitting just .263 through 21 games. But the numbers didn't matter. The Twins had seen all the they needed to see.

In a hotel suite in Seattle, a summit conference was held among the Twins brass to decide what to do, where to go and how to get there.

The meeting consisted of team owner Calvin Griffith, manager Billy Gardner, third-base coach Tom Kelly, long-time Twins coach Rick Stelmaszek and a few other officials.

The situation had become critical in center field as starter Jim Eisenreich had come down with a mysterious illness (later diagnosed as Tourette's Syndrome) and backup Darrell Brown had done nothing to inspire long-term confidence.

Kelly and Stelmaszek, who coached Puckett in the Instructional League, thought he was ready. Others, including Mud Hens manager Ermer thought Puckett could use a little more seasoning in the minors.

Kelly and Stelmaszek admitted they weren't sure if Puckett was ready either, but he had all the tools. He was already a major league fielder and had major league speed. Could he hit big league pitching? That remained to be seen, but they knew he had met every other challenge thrown at him so why not that.

On May 6, 1984, Puckett got the word.

The Mud Hens were on the road in Old Orchard Beach, Maine, outside Portland. Puckett was nearly mad with boredom. For three days, it had rained and Puckett and his roommate had been able to do nothing but watch TV, play cards and eat.

Then came a knock on his door. Standing outside in the driving rain was Ermer, with a smile on his face.

"He looked at me and said, 'Congratulations, kid. You're going to the big show,' " Puckett recounted. " 'The big show', They really do say that in the minors. I jumped up and said, 'Who? Me?' Ermer said, 'No, me. Yeah, you. Congratulations.' "

The Twins wanted Puckett to join them the next day in Anaheim, Calif. for the start of a series with the Angels.

"The first thing I did was get on the phone with my mother," Puckett said. "You know Mom was excited. She called all my brothers and sisters and they all got excited."

For Puckett, the dream had been realized. He played barely two seasons of minor league baseball and he had received the call.

"I was scared to death," he said. "But I also believed I could do the job. They always tell you in baseball, at every level, that if you didn't belong, you wouldn't be here. I was a pretty confident baseball player — always had been — and I believed it."

In just about four years, Puckett had gone from laying carpet in Thunderbirds to making it to the major leagues. It was a dizzying, incredible journey that had seen him succeed at every level.

Puckett had said years before that all he wanted was an opportunity to prove himself and he would do the rest.

He was as good as his word.

Kirby Puckett dives back into first base under the tag of Baltimore Orioles first baseman Eddie Murray during a May, 1985 game. This was Puckett's first full season in the big leagues, after spending barely two seasons in the minors.

CHAPTER FOUR
A MAJOR ACCOMPLISHMENT

Kirby Puckett hit the big leagues with $10 in his pocket and panic in his heart.

It was supposed to run so smoothly, wasn't it? This was the major leagues and everything operated with laser-like precision, didn't it? The Minnesota Twins had summoned him from Class AAA Toledo to play for them so they knew what they were doing, didn't they?

It seemed to make sense from the outside looking in, but it didn't quite happen that way on May 7, 1984, the day Puckett was introduced to the chaotic world of major league baseball.

Puckett, who over the past two seasons had gone from a decent prospect to perhaps the best prospect in the game, figured he'd be spending that season with the Mud Hens, and that was fine with him.

But when the Twins made the decision to bring him up to the big club, everything changed. Now Puckett had to rethink his future and just where he fit into the grand scheme. Supremely confident anyway, he felt he was ready, though he admitted to himself that talking a good game was just a little different than playing a good game.

Now he had his chance.

If he could get where he was supposed to be, that is.

Puckett, who got the call while the Mud Hens were playing in Portland, Maine, was expected to join the Twins that night during Minnesota's West Coast stop with the California Angels.

From Portland, he stopped in Atlanta where his flight was canceled due to aircraft problems.

"A cracked windshield or the defroster isn't working, or something," Puckett grumbled.

For hours, Puckett sat in the Atlanta airport doing a slow burn while his baseball career went on without him.

"I'm sitting around waiting, looking at my watch, worrying. Really worrying," Puckett said. "I've got $10 in my pocket. After a few hours and no plane yet, I'm panicking and don't have any phone number to call. All (Mud Hens' manager) Cal Ermer told me was that someone would meet me at the airport in Anaheim at 4 p.m."

Finally, at 6 p.m., Puckett arrives in California. Of course, no one is there to meet him.

What happened next is another Puckett story that has found its way into Minnesota Twins lore.

Desperate, panicked and uncertain what to do, Puckett decided he had no choice but to hail a cab, even though he only had $10 to his name, and tell the cabby he'd have to wait at the other end to get the rest of his fare. It was a gamble Puckett knew Chicago cabbies wouldn't take but he had no choice but to hope he'd find a Los Angeles cabby who was a trusting sort.

He did.

"I told him I was a minor league ballplayer just called up to the major leagues," Puckett recounted. "I told him I only had $10 with me and that he'd have to wait at the stadium while I went inside to get my meal money to pay him. No problem, he said."

But when Puckett finally reached Anaheim Stadium, the meter read a staggering $60.

Puckett left one bag in the taxi and rushed to the clubhouse door where he introduced himself.

"Oh yeah, Kirby Puckett," the doorman said. "Come on in."

Even in his agitated state, Puckett was impressed.

"In one day I'd gone from 'Who are you?' to 'Oh yeah, come on in.' "

Finally Puckett tracked down Twins traveling secretary Mike Robertson and Puckett recounted his tale of woe to the amused official. Robertson said the Twins would pay for the cab, handed Puckett a $100 bill and the relieved ballplayer gave the trusting cabby a $25 tip.

That's how it began.

The baseball team Puckett joined that day bore little resemblance

AP/Wide World Photos

Puckett slides safely into second under the tag of Boston Red Sox second baseman Marty Barrett in an August, 1985 contest. Puckett hit .288 that first season, stole a career-high 21 bases and also hit a career-best 13 triples.

to the team that would win two World Series titles in a four-year span. Simply, the Minnesota Twins were a struggling franchise with little fan enthusiasm, few quality players and a dubious future at best.

Disgruntled Calvin Griffith still owned the team but was desperately looking to sell it. Carl Pohlad, a local businessman, appeared interested and a deal was close, though far from done. Fans were staying away from the Metrodome in droves and the Twin Cities business community was buying tickets at bulk rates to help close the escape clause Griffith had in the Metrodome lease that would allow him to move the team to Tampa-St. Petersburg, Fla.

None of that mattered to Puckett on that May evening in California. He had reached the big leagues and he meant to make the most of the opportunity.

"We weren't looking for a star when Puckett came up from the minors," said Twins coach Rick Stelmaszek, one of Puckett's early admirers. "We were just looking for a warm body to replace (former center fielder) Darrell Brown."

They found one.

But as spectacular as Puckett had been in the minors, his call-up to the Twins was as much a sign of desperation as anything.

"We needed players," then-manager Billy Gardner said. "I was losing 100 games a year and Kirby was outstanding in the minor leagues. You're talking about a rookie. You figure, what the hell, he's going to fall on his face. But he was great."

Puckett recalled his first experiences with the Twins, the team he would give everything he had for the ensuing 12 years.

"When I stepped on the field, I saw more people in the stands for batting practice than came to a lot of the Mud Hens games," he said. "I was going from a stadium with eight or nine thousand seats to one with fifty, sixty, seventy thousand. You can ask any ballplayer and he'll tell you about that first view of the stands as a major leaguer. It's a thrill. But me — I was frantic again."

Because Puckett arrived so late from the airport, Gardner had to scrap his original plan of starting Puckett in center field that night. Instead, Puckett immediately grabbed a bat and dove into his first batting practice as a major leaguer.

"I hit the ball pretty solidly," he said. "Nothing spectacular."

That's when he finally met Gardner.

"You look a little jet-lagged," Gardner said.

"Not really, coach, I'm ready to go," Puckett responded. "I'm a little tired, but I'm ready."

But Gardner gave Puckett a break, telling him he'd watch the game from the bench that night and then take over in center the following night.

Several Twins looked at Puckett in amazement and wondered if the Twins organization had truly lost its mind. Here was a 5-8, 175-pounder with a physique more suited to bowling than major league baseball, but once they got to know the irrepressible newcomer, they were hooked.

"I congratulated him while he was getting dressed," said former Twins infielder Ron Washington, who became a close friend. "I wished him all the luck in the world. Once he got on the field, though, he didn't need any luck."

Puckett went around the locker room introducing himself to the other players and calling all of them "mister."

"I'd never met a lot of these guys," Puckett said. "They were all big and confident and veterans, practically. Sure I called them mister."

And two of the Twins veteran stars — Kent Hrbek and Tom Brunansky — also had the two numbers Puckett had hoped to wear, 14 (Ernie Banks' number) and 24 (Willie Mays'), respectively. So he decided to stick with the number he'd been given just prior to batting practice — 34.

"It suits me fine," he said.

Finally, after watching his first game from the comfort of the dugout, Puckett's chance came on May 8, 1984.

Prior to the game, a nervous Puckett sat in the dugout when Angels star Reggie Jackson sat down next to him and shook his hand.

"You're name's Puckett, right?" he said.

"Yes, Mr. Jackson," he said. "Nice to meet you Mr. Jackson."

"It looks like you hit them a long way," Jackson said.

"No, just a few singles," replied Puckett.

With that Jackson roared, "Another singles hitter. What am I doing shaking your hand, then?"

He would learn soon enough.

Puckett's first major league at-bat came against Jim Slaton and on the first pitch (what else?) he hit a rocket between short and third. Shortstop Dick Schofield back-handed the ball smartly and

AP/Wide World Photos

Here, Puckett's not quite so fortunate on the base paths as he's rung up by Orioles second baseman Juan Bonilla on an attempted steal during a May, 1986 game.

threw out the streaking Puckett by a step.

The play caught Puckett's attention and offered stark evidence of just how different this game was from the minors.

"I thought, 'Man, in Triple A, that's a hit,' " Puckett said. "If this is how it's going to be in the big leagues, I'm in trouble. I'm in big trouble. I need those infield hits."

Undaunted, Puckett, again facing Slaton, showed the same aggressiveness in his second at-bat and drilled a single to center.

"It was awesome," Washington said. "It was a pea right up the middle."

But before Puckett could celebrate too long, third-base coach Tom Kelly flashed the steal sign and Puckett swiped second with ease. Shortly after that, he was driven home by John Castino and Puckett had his first big-league run.

He was far from finished.

He batted three more times and pounded out three more singles, ending the night four-for-five, just the ninth player in major league history to get four hits in his big league debut.

The next day, Puckett was sitting in the dugout prior to the game when Jackson approached him again. From that stage on, it appeared Jackson had assumed the role as Puckett's teacher, with the young outfielder a willing, voracious pupil. Jackson told Puckett about the things that never showed up in the boxscore, about what it meant to be a major leaguer, what it would take to stay a major leaguer and what it would take to be successful.

"In the minor leagues, you get a pitch to hit every at-bat," Jackson told Puckett. "Here, you're going to get only one a game and you have to make sure you don't let that one go by."

The two became close friends and, in time, Puckett figures to join his mentor in the Hall of Fame.

Another important figure in Puckett's big-league development was Washington, the 32-year-old utility infielder who was the oldest Twins player in 1984.

"The Twins thought I could learn a lot from Ron," Puckett said. "And I did. We talked mostly baseball for hours and when I might get a little negative, which wasn't very often, Ron was always positive. And that's one reason I try to be that way with rookies now."

Washington, who roomed with Puckett in 1985, also convinced Puckett not to be so obsessed with talented major league pitching.

"Obviously, it was better than anything I'd ever faced," he said. "But Ron convinced me to concentrate on my hitting, not their pitching. You can't be passive at the plate. It's death. I learned a lot from Ron about being positive, being aggressive, never getting the idea that things at the plate are never out of my control."

It was a philosophy Puckett had always tried to live by anyway, but Washington was able to drive it home more convincingly than anyone else.

Washington also schooled Puckett on other subjects as well — from when to get to the ballpark for batting practice, to eating habits, to how to approach the game itself.

"He taught me how things should be done on and off the field," Puckett said. If a guy had poor form or lousy hustle, he'd say, 'Don't play like that.' He was that blunt. He taught me most of what I knew at the time about being a major league ballplayer, not just a ballplayer."

As it turned out, that season laid the groundwork for what would become a Twins world championship team just three years later. It was a season that saw the Twins tied for first in the American League West in July and saw them stay in contention all season.

But after blowing that 10-0 lead to the Indians late in the season, Minnesota never recovered and finished tied for second with California, three games behind the Kansas City Royals.

Puckett ended up hitting .296, with no home runs. In fact, of his 165 hits that season, 148 were singles. He also led the AL with 16 assists from the outfield.

Puckett finished third in the balloting for AL Rookie of the Year behind Seattle's Alvin Davis and Mark Langston, and was named to most of the postseason all-rookie teams.

All in all, Puckett couldn't complain about his first taste of the major leagues. But, as he soon discovered, it would only get better.

By 1985, Puckett was entrenched with the Twins. He had proven the year before that the faith shown in him throughout his stint in the minors was well placed. And, as a result, he had taken his last bus ride, stayed in his last two-bit motel and seen his last minor league ballpark.

Though the Twins didn't match their exciting run for a pennant that year, Puckett continued to evolve and learn as a major-leaguer. He posted a .288 batting average, which he considered a profound disappointment and he hit four home runs and added 74 runs batted in along with 29 doubles and 13 triples. Not bad numbers at all for a guy who considered himself little more than a singles hitter.

But if there was a highlight that season for Puckett, it came on April 22 when he hit his first big-league homer, a 340-foot effort that barely landed in the second row of seats in left field at the Metrodome. For trivia buffs, the dinger was hit against Seattle Mariners left-hander Matt Young.

And while it may not have been a Ruthian shot, it meant the world to Puckett. But, this being the big time, Puckett found himself hip-deep in an age-old tradition — the old silent treatment.

It's traditional that when a non-home run hitter puts one out, his teammates stay on the bench, acting as if nothing had happened. No slaps on the back, no hugs, no high-fives. And, after nearly 600 at-bats with the Twins, Puckett was a perfect candidate.

Puckett recounted the exchange in his book.

"I wasn't so naive that I didn't know about the silent treatment," he said. "But a couple of minutes went by and still nobody had said anything."

Exasperated, Puckett finally cracked.

"Geez, guys, weren't you watching?" he beseeched. "Don't you know the Puck finally hit a homer?"

With that, his teammates relented and congratulated him on what would be the first of his many taters for the Twins.

Unknown to Puckett at the time, a 13-year-old kid from nearby Wayzata, Minn., Bobby Hatcher, made a head-long dive to grab that souvenir homer. Few others may have known, or really cared, about who some guy named Kirby Puckett was.

But Bobby Hatcher did.

"He was already one of my favorite players," Hatcher said, many years after the event. "There was just something about him. He was this short guy I viewed as some kind of underdog trying to make it, and I could relate to that. And at the time, nobody thought of him as a home run hitter, so I was thinking this might be one of the few he would hit in the major leagues."

After the game, Hatcher sought out Puckett and gave him the ball. In return, Puckett presented Hatcher with a ball of his own, signed "To Bobby; best wishes, Kirby Puckett."

Puckett was appreciative, in fact, he told the kid to come back a few days later and he'd have a bat to give him.

But when Hatcher showed, Puckett had no bat to give him.

"You could tell he felt bad," Hatcher said. "So he told me to come over to his car and he opened his trunk and said 'Let me see what I have in here.' "

He eventually uncovered an old glove that he gave to the 13-year-old kid who had retrieved his first major league homer.

"I'll never forget that night," Hatcher said. "And to see how his career developed the way it did, and to see how much he came to mean to everybody just adds to the whole thing."

As for giving up what would eventually amount to a impressive collector's item, Hatcher had no second thoughts.

"To a guy like that, you don't mind giving up something that precious," he said. "If it was a jerk like Albert Belle, maybe. But why would you deny Kirby?"

It was around that time as well that the nickname "Puck" became part of the Twins lexicon.

With his unique physique (which had expanded to nearly 200 pounds on a 5-8 body) and shiny bald head, nicknames abounded for Puckett.

Brunswick, after the bowling ball, got a brief run. So did Stub, Fire Hydrant, Fire Plug, Buddha, Pit Bull, Cannonball, Cannonball Head, Bucket Head, Hockey Puck and some others that probably shouldn't be mentioned. But the name Puck eventually won out.

Yet 1985 was a season of change, not only for Puckett, but for the Twins.

After their impressive showing in 1984 when they fell just short of the Kansas City Royals, the Twins were picked by many to win the AL West. But it wasn't coming together and by mid-June the Twins were in danger of falling out of sight in the division race.

So, as is always the case when a team sputters, the manager gets the blame and in this instance, Gardner was fired.

"I liked Billy Gardner because he took a chance on me the previous year," Puckett said.

As Gardner was clearing out his locker and heading out the door, he stopped and told Puckett he'd be watching his career with great interest.

"I appreciated that," he said. "I think he really meant it."

In Gardner's place stepped Ray Miller, the pitching coach of the Baltimore Orioles, who had no major-league managing experience.

But while the Twins weren't going anywhere in the American League that season, Puckett used batting practice to experiment and what came from those experiments drastically changed what kind of hitter Puckett became.

"A lot of my 199 hits that season had been to right field (the opposite field)," Puckett said. "I'd always had an inside-out stroke, taking the ball to right field."

But late in the season, teammates began to tease Puckett about being nothing more than right-field hitter, a singles hitter. And even though it was a description Puckett agreed with, he still found himself getting annoyed by the razzing.

Deep down, he thought, he could hit home runs. He'd never been in a position to have to do it before, but, suddenly, Puckett accepted the challenge of his jeering teammates.

During one batting session, Puckett proceeded to hit 10 straight balls out of the park. And not 340-footers either — legitimate, big-league bombs.

He changed his frame of mind from hitting the opposite way to just get on base to swinging for the fences and making things happen.

"It gave me something to think about," he said.

He also had something else to think about — a new contract.

His rookie season, Puckett made the standard $40,000 (that was still a lot of money then, you know). And though he had next to no leverage in the game yet, Puckett was given a hefty raise for 1985 — up to $120,000 a year plus $10,000 in incentives.

"I had to adjust to the fact that, from now on, my financial standing would be public knowledge and the subject of debate," he said. "There's nothing I can do about that, but I still don't like it."

After the 1985 season, Puckett hired Baltimore agent Ron Shapiro, who also represented high-profile players like the Orioles' Cal Ripken and Eddie Murray.

Puckett and Shapiro have been together ever since.

"I didn't want my negotiations on the front page," Puckett said. "And that's Ron's style too. I have total trust in Ron."

That trust paid quick dividends as Shapiro negotiated yet another raise for Puckett in 1986 — a boost up to $230,000 a year.

"All (Ron) could do was prod the Twins to pay me what was fair," he said. "After starting out at 40 grand, plus the bonus, two years earlier, I was really happy."

But for the money, the Twins expected production and in the 1986 season, they got it.

Puckett's transformation from a singles hitter to power hitter was gradual but dramatic. Yet it was Twins' icon Tony Oliva who had seen something special in Puckett three years earlier when he was Minnesota's roving hitting instructor.

"Even back then he had suggested that I had the body and the power to hit 20 homers a season," Puckett said.

Puckett scoffed at the idea, mainly because he had never envisioned himself in that role and he didn't want to mess up his swing for the sake of the long ball.

But there was another reason.

"It scared me," he said. "Being known as a home run hitter brings a lot more pressure. I didn't know whether I wanted that."

Nonetheless, he attacked spring training that season with a new attitude at the plate. Instead of simply wanting to hit the ball hard somewhere, he wanted to hit the ball out — somewhere.

An off-season weight-lifting regimen helped not only his strength but his bat speed and he also took to lifting his front leg prior to the pitch to help increase his power.

He took the American League by storm.

He was named the league's Player of the Month for April, hitting .389 and belting nine home runs, five more than he'd had in his entire major league career before that.

One of those especially stayed in Puckett's mind.

It came in one of baseball cathedrals, New York's Yankee Stadium. After two long fly outs to deep center, manager Ray Miller told Puckett, "This park's too big for you." Stung by that, Puckett took a knee-high Joe Niekro fastball in the seventh inning and deposited it 500 feet into the hallowed monuments in center.

When Miller tried to shake his hand, Puckett jokingly refused.

"Too big for me, huh?" he told Miller. "There's your 'too big.' "

But Puckett admitted he may not have been entirely kidding with Miller, who had questioned his ability earlier.

"I'm sensitive when someone tells me I can't do something," he said.

But, after that monstrous blast, Miller never did it again.

It was a bittersweet season for Puckett, who watched his numbers soar while the Twins plummeted in the standings.

The 1986 campaign also signaled the start of a stunning power surge by Puckett. In his first season and a half, Puckett hit just four home runs. But he opened that season on fire, hitting seven homers in his first 19 games and chalking up a staggering .700 slugging percentage. For the season, he hit 31 home runs, which proved to be a career high for him.

Puckett was never too busy to visit with an old friend, before or during the game. Here, he chats with former Cleveland Indians' second baseman Carlos Baerga during a break in the action.

Kirby relaxes prior to a game. Though he's boisterous and fun-loving before a game, during the game he's all business.

The trademark leg kick. Puckett developed this early in his major-league career to help him increase his bat speed. He never altered it throughout his years in the big leagues.

Puckett clowns with one of his best friends in baseball, Twins first baseman Kent Hrbek. Between the two of them, they may have formed the most enduring and recognizable duo the franchise has ever known.

It wasn't always fun and games with Puckett. Case in point, he's woofing at the home plate umpire during a 1992 game against the Milwaukee Brewers.

Kirby Puckett also formed a tight friendship with fellow outfielder Shane Mack, a younger player in whom he saw a kindred spirit. And Mack flourished under Puckett's guidance.

Puckett acknowledges a sold-out Metrodome during the Twins celebration of their 1991 World Series title.

It's utter bedlam after Game Seven of the 1991 World Series as the Twins beat the Atlanta Braves, four games to three. Here, Puckett is interviewed immediately after Minnesota's scintillating 10th-inning win.

At a Minnesota Twins family day, Kirby Puckett poses with the most important people in his life: his wife Tonya and his kids Catherine (right, named after Kirby's mom) and Kirby Jr.

Photo by Richard Orndorf

This was not an altogether uncommon sight for Twins fans. Puckett hit 207 career home runs, not bad for a guy who claimed he was not a power hitter.

Photo by Richard Orndorf

You must be popular when you get a street named after you. Such was the case in 1996 when Kirby Puckett Place in Minneapolis was unveiled by its namesake.

Even in his darkest moment, Kirby Puckett had a smile on his face. During his retirement announcement on July 12, 1996, Puckett waves to friends in the crowd while his wife Tonya watches.

Puckett limbers up as he prepares to throw out the ceremonial first pitch on "Kirby Puckett Night" at the Metrodome on Sept. 7, 1996.

The man known as Puck.

He was playing so well that Puckett was making a serious run at earning a starting spot on the American League All-Star team, the first Twin to do that since Roy Smalley in 1979. In early July, though, just as the voting was shutting down, it appeared Puckett had fallen short to three of baseball's established outfield stars — Dave Winfield, Reggie Jackson and Rickey Henderson.

But all that changed when Puckett, sitting in the dugout during Minnesota's game in Detroit, was approached by Miller and informed that he had indeed beaten out Henderson in a late surge to earn the starting spot in center for the American League.

It was Puckett's first All-Star appearance. It would not be his last.

Puckett, who was hitting .340 with 16 homers at the break, was given the leadoff spot by AL manager Dick Howser and promptly stroked the first pitch (what else?) up the middle for a single.

"My real surprise was that I wasn't nervous at the plate," Puckett said.

He was the only American Leaguer to play the entire game and was told by Howser afterward that he knew the junior circuit would win if Puckett played the whole game.

And it did, 3-2, as Puckett went one-for-three with a walk.

Puckett's drastic improvement at the plate in terms of producing power obviously didn't go unnoticed by Miller, who, shortly after the All-Star Game, stunned Puckett by telling him he would become Minnesota's No. 3 hitter.

A lifetime leadoff hitter with no history of hitting for power had suddenly been moved from his comfortable spot to one that demanded he produce runs.

One of the highlights of Puckett's career was earning his first-ever All-Star berth in 1986. Here, he slides safely into third with a stolen base after San Francisco Giant Chris Brown lets the ball slip away. Puckett went 1 for 3 with that stolen base and a walk for the American League. That also marked the first of 10 straight All-Star appearances for Puckett.

"I wasn't sure I was up to it," Puckett admitted. "I'm not exaggerating when I say how unsure I was about that decision. In my mind, the change they were asking of me was drastic. I was finally getting comfortable in the majors, confident of my abilities as a leadoff hitter, and now this. I was honored and scared at the same time."

But Puckett made the most of the opportunity. In fact, he ended up battling two of baseball's purest hitters — Boston's Wade Boggs and New York's Don Mattingly — for the AL batting championship.

And though he finished third with a still glittering .333 average, Puckett, who also did a lot of hitting from the No. 1 spot again, learned just how difficult it was to stay consistent at the plate during an entire season.

"At that level, one hit a game is not enough," he said. "The jump from being a .300 hitter to a .333 hitter is just incredible."

Through much of the season, Puckett appeared to be a serious candidate for the league MVP though he eventually finished sixth. It was a situation he didn't think twice about.

"I don't worry about stuff I can't control," he said. "I don't know where I learned that, but I'm pretty good at it."

It was also a season that saw the foundation being laid for the Twins future.

On September 12, as the Twins were staggering toward the end of a miserable season, Miller was fired and replaced by third-base coach Tom Kelly, squelching rumors that the mercurial Billy Martin would be brought back.

"I think it was immediately clear to everyone that Tom Kelly wasn't just another manager," Puckett said.

Puckett finished 1986 with 31 home runs, making him the first player in major league history to hit more than 30 homers after going more than 500 at-bats without a home run in a previous season. Of his 223 hits, a remarkable one-third had been for extra bases — 37 doubles, six triples and 31 homers. The year before, only one in four of his hits had been for extra bases.

"I couldn't have imagined in my wildest dreams that kind of extra-base production," he said.

But while the personal numbers were encouraging, Puckett was ready for team success. He knew the pieces were in place for the Twins to not only be competitive, but to be a title contender. Minnesota had power in Kent Hrbek, Gary Gaetti, Tom Brunansky and Puckett. The pitching was anchored by starter Frank Viola and closer Jeff Reardon and the off-season acquisition of leadoff hitter Dan Gladden allowed Puckett to move to the No. 3 spot in the batting order permanently.

There was no reason — not one, Puckett thought— that the Twins could not be a power in the American League.

He thought 1987 might be the season the Twins finally proved it.

He was right.

Two similar scenes, two different years, the same result. In each, taken four years apart, Kirby Puckett, wearing an aviator's cap, celebrates during a World Series victory parade through downtown Minneapolis. But notice that in the first one, taken in 1987, Tonya Puckett doesn't look exactly thrilled to be there. That's because the crush of fans to honor Puckett and the Twins nearly turned into a riot. The second, in 1991, was handled better and both Kirby and Tonya seem to be enjoying this one.

CHAPTER FIVE
TWIN KILLINGS

The Minnesota Twins had been nothing special for years.

They had made occasional runs, played some good baseball, caught a few notices along the way. But, really, since losing to the Los Angeles Dodgers in the 1965 World Series, the franchise had been adrift in a sea of mediocrity and there was really no reason for that to change as the 1987 season dawned.

But something was different.

"I looked at our lineup and knew we were a good team," Puckett recalled.

It was a team that seemed to have everything necessary to challenge for a pennant. But looking like a contender and proving to be one are two different things. And the Twins knew they had some serious baggage — 21 years with no pennant — to unload.

Puckett and teammate Tom Brunansky, another key member of the '87 World Series team, rejoice after beating the Cardinals.

But they wasted little time showing they would have to be taken seriously.

It started, really, with opening day at the Metrodome against another rising AL West power, the Oakland Athletics.

The Twins won it in the bottom of the 10th and Puckett was instrumental on both offense and defense. He finished with a home run, double and a single and in the top of the 10th with the game tied at 4-4, he leaped over the center field wall and took a potential home run away from Mickey Tettleton. He did the same thing the next night to Reggie Jackson.

Though long noted for his offensive prowess, Puckett has probably never really gotten the credit he deserved as a defensive player.

"That's my land out there," said Puckett, a six-time Gold Glove winner who finished with a sparkling .989 field percentage. "And don't you go messing with it with your doubles and triples and homers that barely clear the wall. You'd better get the ball way over. I've always said that I'd rather take away a homer than hit one."

Under the firm but restrained hand of Tom Kelly, the Twins were starting to live up to expectations. The offense was as good as advertised. The defense was playing superbly. And the unknown factor, the pitching staff, was doing its job. As a result, the Twins found themselves entrenched in first place by the All-Star break.

Puckett was again on fire, hitting .340, and though he wasn't voted onto the All Star team as a starter, still made his second straight midseason classic. It proved to be a less-than-memorable affair though, as he struck out three times, leading to a period of uncharacteristically uneven hitting for Puckett.

Kirby Puckett waves to the Metrodome crowd after accepting the award as the American League top hitter in 1989. Puckett's .339 average was the highest by a right-handed hitter to win the honor since California's Alex Johnson in 1970. He also led the majors in batting, hits and multi-hit games.

Then came an August weekend at Milwaukee County Stadium that Puckett called the best series of his professional life.

Puckett admitted he went into the series struggling at the plate.

"I was lunging at the ball," he said. "I was swinging not just at bad pitches, which is my habit, but at terrible pitches."

Before Saturday's game, Puckett and hitting coach Tony Oliva sat down on the tarp along the left field line to discuss Puckett's woes. But before anyone could say anything, Puckett picked up a bat that was lying next to him and he was amazed how good it felt in his hands.

Puckett turned to Oliva and smiled.

"Tony, I feel great today," he said. "Check me out today. I don't know what it is."

He would soon find out.

In the game Saturday, Puckett went four-for-five with two home runs and two singles. But that was just a prelude to Sunday's fireworks.

"I told Tony on Sunday I felt the same as I had on Saturday," Puckett said. "I could feel I was still in that zone."

Puckett was already five-for-five when he came to bat late in the game against Brewers closer Dan Plesac.

"He throws a fastball low and away — a tough, tough pitch," Puckett said. "And I don't know what happened but I kicked my leg and swung."

The result was a bullet into the right center field seats that sealed the win for the Twins and put them back in first place over Oakland.

Photo by Richard Orndorf

Puckett is introduced on opening day 1988, the first game back since the Twins won their first-ever World Series over the St. Louis Cardinals.

He finished the day six-for-six with two home runs, two doubles and two singles, culminating a two-day, 10-for-11, four-homer blitzkrieg. The 14 total bases on Sunday also set a club record and the 10 hits in consecutive nine-inning games set an American League record.

"Every ball I hit that weekend was hard," he said. "I've never felt that way since, and if I never do again, that's all right because I felt that way once."

It marked Puckett's renaissance and offered a clear signal that the Twins would be in the pennant race for the long haul.

With a week left in the season, the Twins clinched the AL West with a win over the Texas Rangers and though a five-game losing streak ensued (dropping the Twins to a final 85-77 record) Puckett didn't care. He knew the press was making a lot out of the fact that Minnesota's record was the worst among division champs (and just ninth-best in baseball that year) but Puckett had a simple response: It was the best record in the AL West and that's all that mattered.

The Twins went into the playoffs against what was generally considered the best team in baseball, the Detroit Tigers, who had won a major-league best 98 games.

It wasn't supposed to be a contest. And it wasn't.

Minnesota jumped on the Tigers in Game One at the Metrodome, winning 8-5 behind Gary Gaetti's two home runs and Tom Brunansky's three runs batted in. The victory was especially important to the Twins for two reasons: The first was that it came against Tigers' ace Doyle Alexander, who had gone 9-0 since coming over to Detroit in an August trade.

Photo by Richard Orndorf

The long and the short of it: Kent Hrbek and Kirby Puckett.

"We proved he was human," manager Tom Kelly said.

The second, more important reason, was that it proved to the rest of baseball that the Twins were no fluke, that they belonged in the ALCS no matter their record.

Puckett went one-for-four in that game, but it was a big hit as he doubled home Dan Gladden to tie the score in the eighth inning. Designated hitter Don Baylor followed with a single that scored Puckett and put Minnesota ahead for good.

In Game Two, the Twins beat Detroit's other superb hurler, Jack Morris, 6-3. Puckett was hitless in four trips but Gladden again had a strong game, delivering a crucial two-run single.

The series shifted to Detroit's Tiger Stadium for the next three games. Although they trailed 0-2, Detroit had to feel confident since the Twins were a miserable 29-52 on the road and had won just nine road games since the All-Star break.

And Game Three seemed to drive that point home as the Tigers posted a 7-6 win that was keyed by journeyman Pat Sheridan. Though he'd had just five hits in his last 68 at-bats, Sheridan belted a two-run homer that sent the Tigers on their way. Puckett again struggled at the plate, going zero for five.

But it was impossible to keep him down forever and in Game Four, Puckett erupted with two hits, including a home run, and scored twice as Minnesota reasserted control with a 5-3 win.

"My teammates know it's just a matter of time," Puckett said. "I just play hard and let the chips fall where they may."

Leading 3-1 in the series, the Twins ended the thing quickly, pounding the Tigers, 9-5, the next afternoon to clinch the ALCS and earn a trip to the World Series.

A four-run second inning, keyed by Brunansky's two-run double, did most of the damage and Gaetti, named the series Most Valuable Player, belted home runs in his first two at-bats. Puckett went two-for-six and drove in a run.

Minnesota's dominating performance left Tigers' manager Sparky Anderson shaking his head.

"I've never seen a club come in with so much desire," he said.

But it was far from over.

The Twins opponent in the World Series was the St. Louis Cardinals, who survived a rugged seven-game series against the San Francisco Giants. Once again, the Twins were the underdogs.

Minnesota, in front of 55,171 fans at the Metrodome, wasted little time jumping on the Cards and starter Joe Magrane. A Gladden grand slam sparked a seven-run fourth inning and the Twins rolled to a 10-1 win in Game One.

Frank Viola got the victory, throwing eight solid innings. Puckett started the Series quietly, with one hit in five trips.

The Twins kept up the barrage in Game Two, smacking St. Louis 8-4 behind catcher Tim Laudner's two-run single and 420-foot home run. Puckett again did little, going one for four with a run scored.

The World Series shifted to Busch Stadium in St. Louis and the results were not pretty for the Twins.

The Cardinals pitching staff shut down Minnesota's mighty bats, holding the Twins to five runs and 18 hits in three games as St. Louis won three straight to take command. Puckett really struggled, managing just three hits in 11 trips to the plate.

"We were hopping mad after that showing," Puckett said. "No way this team gets 18 hits in three games. I was mad, for sure, and took extra batting practice before game six."

It had been a frustrating series for Puckett, who admitted he had fallen into the trap the St. Louis pitchers had set for him. Knowing he was a hitter who would chase less than perfect pitches, the Cardinals obliged, throwing lots of off-speed junk way off the plate and expecting Puckett to go after it in his impatience to get a hit. It worked.

So, before Game Six, Puckett took the unusual step of watching video of himself trying to hit Cardinal pitching. It was an eye-opening experience.

Back at the Metrodome, Puckett was ready for Cards' veteran John Tudor. On his first trip to the plate and Gladden on second, Puckett tried patience — not normally one of his strong suits. But it worked this time, as he drilled an RBI single to left.

He finished four-for-four, including a walk, four runs scored, a stolen base and an RBI that helped the Twins even the series with an 11-5 win.

In Game Seven, Puckett again played a key role. With the game tied 2-2 in the fifth, Cardinals manager Whitey Herzog replaced the starter Magrane with hard-throwing right-hander Danny Cox. But Puckett was ready and, with Greg Gagne on second, his ringing double to right center put the Twins up for good.

With Minnesota on top 4-2, Puckett recalled trotting out to center to start the ninth inning.

"I had never been as nervous, not even in my first game in the majors three years earlier," he said. "And I've never been anywhere near that nervous since. For the first and last time in my career, I was pleading that the ball not be hit to me. I was terrified I'd make the critical mistake."

Naturally, the first hitter hit a short fly that Puckett camped under and handled easily. Then came the final two outs and the Minnesota Twins had brought home their first championship.

Puckett had another glorious season, hitting .332 with 28 homers and 32 doubles. He also finished third in the MVP balloting, trailing just Toronto's George Bell and Detroit's Alan Trammell.

Puckett had also reached the point in his career where he was eligible for arbitration, the bizarre dance in which a player submits a figure he believes he's worth while the club submits a figure it believes he's worth. After a hearing in which much dirty laundry is normally unveiled, an arbitrator decides on one figure or the other. Somebody is usually unhappy.

"I wanted my organization to be fair," said Puckett, who also desperately wanted to avoid a nasty, public confrontation.

The Twins came in with a figure of $930,000 per season while Puckett's agent, Ron Shapiro, came up with $1.35 million. It was a wide, potentially damaging, gulf.

Yet on the day of the arbitration hearing, Twins' GM Andy McPhail and Shapiro decided to go for a walk and talk it over. About an hour later they returned with a figure of $1.09 million, a number Puckett jumped at. Kirby Puckett was officially a millionaire, the sixth on the Minnesota Twins roster.

It was a long way from the Robert Taylor Homes on Chicago's south side.

The only problem with winning a World Series, though, is that you're expected to do it again. For the Twins, 1987 was a season of vindication. No one had expected them to win and it was that perceived lack of respect that drove them.

In 1988, that wasn't the case, which pointed out the ultimate irony of baseball. That year, the Twins were probably an even better team than they were when they beat the Cards in the World Series.

They won 91 games, six more than the year before, yet they finished far behind the awesome Oakland A's in the AL West, who won 104 games.

Over the next three seasons, Puckett maintained his consistent numbers. In 1988, as the Twins were again sputtering for an identity, Puckett had his best season to date as a major-leaguer.

He hit .356, the best by an American League right-handed hitter since Joe DiMaggio's .357 in 1941. He hit 24 home runs and knocked in 121 runs, and became just the fourth major-leaguer to have 1,000 hits in his first five seasons joining Rod Carew as the only Twin to ever hit .300, have 200 hits, score 100 runs and drive in 100 runs in the same season.

"The simple truth is that I was on the whole year," he said. "You throw it and I'd hit it."

Amazingly, Puckett still didn't win the batting title that season as Boston's Wade Boggs got him again, this time hitting .366.

Boggs and Puckett became friends soon after that. Yet neither can begin to understand the philosophy about hitting the other guy has.

"I'm so spontaneous and he's so mechanical," Puckett said. "He takes pitches right down the middle. I could never do that. I try not to worry about my average. I think about hits. If I get the hits, the average will come."

And both continued to come for Puckett, especially in 1989 when he finally got the best of Boggs and won the AL batting title with a .339 average. He also led the league in hits with 215. And in the fall of '89, the Twins rewarded Puckett with a three-year, $9 million contract that made him the highest-paid player in the game. At least temporarily.

A few days later, Rickey Henderson signed a four-year, $12 million contract with Oakland and, before much longer, players were signing for a lot more than Puckett got.

Asked if he was resentful, Puckett said no.

"I signed my contract and I would stick by it without regrets," he said.

Unfortunately for Puckett, that big deal followed perhaps his worst year in baseball as he hit "only" .298 in 1990, a season he considered an abject failure. As well, the Twins finished 74-88 and last in the AL West.

But 1991 was an entirely different story.

Ironically, Puckett, who gained something approaching immortality for his center field play in the World Series later that year, started the season in right field as part of a grand experiment that was his idea originally.

Convinced he'd lost a step over the years, Puckett suggested to manager Tom Kelly that he move to right field, with youngster

Shane Mack going to center, Dan Gladden staying in left and another promising kid, Pedro Munoz, filling in where needed.

Kelly agreed and Puckett threw himself into his new position during spring training.

He stayed there early into the season before Kelly approached him and told him the grand experiment was over.

"Just tell me where you want to play," Kelly said.

Puckett fumbled for an answer before Kelly asked him again: "Where do you want to play?"

"Well, center field," Puckett responded.

"Then that's where you play," Kelly said.

Puckett was back where he belonged and the Twins were off and running.

Still, even though he hit .319 that season, Puckett admitted 1991 may have been his toughest year hitting.

"I just never saw the ball real well," he said. "I had one hot streak in July but I never felt I carried the Twins, not for a single week. I took extra BP (batting practice), then I took extra extra BP. I worked on keeping my shoulder in, keeping my head still, timing my high leg kick. But I always felt a little out of sync."

Somehow, it was enough, and along with the nucleus of Kent Hrbek, Greg Gagne, Rick Aguilera, the newly acquired outfielder Chili Davis, rookie second baseman Chuck Knoblauch and veteran warhorse pitcher Jack Morris, the Twins had enough to be a contender again.

The key to the Twins' season was a torrid stretch from June 1 to June 16 when Minnesota won 15 straight to move from 5 $\frac{1}{2}$ games behind Oakland to a half-game ahead. It was a lead the Twins wouldn't lose. They won the American League West with a 95-67 record and finished eight games ahead of the Chicago White Sox.

Though the Twins had gone from worst to first in just one season, Puckett was convinced it wasn't an accurate picture.

"We never thought we were a last-place club in 1990," he said.

They proved it '91.

For the second time in five years the Twins were back in the ALCS, this time facing the best of the East, the Toronto Blue Jays.

The series opened at the raucous Metrodome and the Twins bolted to a 5-0 lead behind Morris and seemed ready to cruise. Toronto battled back and closed to within 5-4 before journeyman reliever Carl Willis shut the Jays down with two-plus innings of superb pitching.

Davis led the way with two RBI and Puckett started slowly by going hitless in four at-bats.

By this point, the Twins had developed an aura at the Metrodome, having won six straight postseason games in the place affectionately (and otherwise) known as the "Humpdome."

But that streak came to an end in Game Two as the Blue Jays, behind rookie right-hander Juan Guzman, shut down the Twins, 5-2. Puckett made a little noise, going one-for-four with an RBI.

Game Three saw the series move to Toronto's cavernous SkyDome but Minnesota took the momentum back as Mike Pagliarulo, written off by most teams, hit a stunning pinch-hit homer in the 10th inning off Mike Timlin for the 3-2 win.

There was more good news for the Twins. Puckett was beginning to heat up with a two-for-five performance that included a double and an RBI.

He was even better in Game Four, sparking a four-run fourth inning with a solo homer off Todd Stottlemyre. He also added a sacrifice fly and went three-for-four with two runs scored and two runs batted in as Minnesota rolled, 9-3.

The Twins put the series away in Game Five and again, Puckett lit the fuse. His solo home run in the first got Minnesota rolling and he went three-for-five with two runs and two RBI. The Twins won, 5-3, closing out the ALCS. Puckett, with his nine hits, two homers and six runs batted in, was named the series Most Valuable Player.

"At the start of the series, I wasn't swinging well but that was blown out of proportion," Puckett said. "I just kept swinging."

The Twins awaited the winner of the Pittsburgh Pirates — Atlanta Braves NLCS, a series that ran seven games and was deemed perhaps the most dramatic in baseball history.

But the historians hadn't seen anything yet.

When the Braves overtook Pittsburgh in the final game, it set up one of the strangest World Series in baseball history — pitting two teams that had finished last in their division the year before.

It might not have sounded like much on paper, but it produced some epic October baseball.

The Series started routinely enough in Minneapolis with a methodical 5-2 Twins victory, keyed by Gagne's three-run homer and a solo shot by Kent Hrbek. Puckett, not surprisingly, was nowhere to be found in that game, going hitless in four trips.

Photo by Richard Orndorf

Kirby Puckett's expression says it all as he's showered with champagne and beer after the Twins beat the Toronto Blue Jays to win the 1991 AL pennant and earn a return trip the World Series. Puckett hit .429 with two home runs and six runs batted in and was named the ALCS most valuable player.

Things got interesting in Game Two.

With Minnesota up 2-1 in the top of the third inning. Atlanta's Lonnie Smith reached on an error by rookie third baseman Scott Leius. Ron Gant followed with a single and a bad throw by left fielder Dan Gladden skipped past Leius. Gant rounded first and pitcher Kevin Tapani retrieved the ball and fired to Hrbek at first trying to nab Gant.

What happened next became part of World Series lore.

As the 170-pound Gant dove back to the bag, the 250-pound Hrbek, a huge fan of pro wrestling, lifted Gant off the bag, tagged him and umpire Drew Coble called him out. The Braves couldn't believe it and the Metrodome quaked with excitement.

Hrbek pleaded innocent afterward.

"His momentum carried him into me," he said. "I knew he was going to fall off the bag because that's where his momentum was taking him."

An irate Gant saw it far differently.

"I don't know since when you can just pull a guy off the bag," he said.

Whatever, it shifted momentum and the Twins took a 2-0 series lead with the 3-2 victory. Puckett was hitless in four trips again.

Game Three was in Atlanta's Fulton County Stadium, where Braves fans had not forgotten Hrbek's stunt the previous game. It got so bad that Hrbek received a death threat.

Before pregame introductions, Puckett made a point of searching out Hrbek to make sure he had no other shenanigans in mind.

Puckett connects on a third-inning solo home run off Atlanta's Steve Avery in Game three of the World Series.

"After all, he'd be standing next to me on the foul line during the introductions because I was batting behind him in the lineup," Puckett said. "An unfriendly greeting was guaranteed; if the Braves' fans starting throwing stuff, I'd be in the line of fire."

The Braves downed the Twins, 5-4 in 12 innings, as Mark Lemke delivered a two-out single to score Dave Justice with the game-winner. Puckett did his part with a solo homer.

Game Four was even better as Lemke tripled in the ninth and scored just ahead of Brian Harper's tag after a Jerry Willard sacrifice fly. The Braves' 3-2 win tied the series at 2-2. Puckett added a hit in four at-bats.

Game Five was a disaster for the Twins as Atlanta pounded out 17 hits and crushed Minnesota 14-5. Puckett had a hit and a run in two official trips.

After getting swept in Atlanta, the Twins couldn't wait to get home. But upon entering the clubhouse hours before Game Six, Puckett was concerned about the atmosphere.

"The clubhouse was pretty quiet when I walked in," he recounted in his book. "Too quiet, I thought. Hey, this is the World Series. It's a privilege to play in the World Series, not a chore. Sure our backs were to the wall, but so what? We'd been there against the Cardinals in '87 and ended up popping the corks."

Puckett was particularly animated this day because he knew he needed to be. His team needed him, perhaps more than it had ever needed him before.

That's when Puckett announced that he was going to take charge.

Among Twins fans, this will always and forever be known as "The Catch." Puckett leaped up against the left centerfield wall to rob Atlanta's Ron Gant of at least extra bases if not a home run in Game Six.

"Jump on board, boys," he told them. "I'm going to carry us tonight. Don't even worry about it. Just back me up a little bit and I'll take us to Game Seven."

It was more than an idle boast, although Puckett hadn't yet enjoyed a great series. But he felt a change, something was different and a few hours later, he showed what that was.

It started with what has come to be known in Minnesota as "The Catch."

It came in the third inning, with Atlanta's Terry Pendleton on first base and Ron Gant at the plate.

Gant climbed all over a Scott Erickson fastball and sent it to deep left center.

"After playing more than 500 games in center field in the Metrodome, I know almost instantly whether any ball is going to the warning track, the wall, barely over the wall or way over the wall," Puckett said.

Puckett's first reaction on this wasn't good. He thought it was gone.

But as he sprinted back for it, he realized it wasn't going to go out after all. He reached out to find the wall, timed his jump perfectly and picked the drive off the window pane.

The Metrodome erupted as Gant stood, watching in disbelief.

That could well have been the enduring image of Puckett if not for his heroics a few innings later.

The game was tied at 3-3 in the bottom of the 11th inning when Puckett and his good friend and teammate Al Newman noticed

Later in the game, Puckett added more heroics, smacking a leadoff home run off Charlie Leibrandt to give Minnesota the 4-3, 11th inning win. For the game, Puckett went 3 for 4 with three RBI and two runs scored. He also made good on his pregame pep talk in which he told his disconsolate teammates that they could hop on his back and he'd carry them to victory.

left-hander Charlie Leibrandt warming up in the bullpen.

Both Puckett and Newman recalled a time four years earlier when Leibrandt was pitching for the Royals. In that game, Newman started a rally with a double and Puckett, Gary Gaetti and Hrbek had followed with home runs to break the game open.

With that memory fresh in his head, Puckett turned to Newman and said simply, "I can hit this guy."

As Leibrandt went to the mound to start the inning, Newman said to Puckett, "Puck, here comes your man."

Puckett was the leadoff hitter in the inning and, even though he hit left-handers extremely well, Braves' manager Bobby Cox, nonetheless, went with Leibrandt.

On a 2-1 count, Leibrandt threw a changeup high in the strike zone and Puckett crushed it over the left field wall for a home run that gave Minnesota the 4-3 win and new World Series life.

"I was almost hyperventilating during the celebration," Puckett said.

Later, he reflected on the remarkable performance.

"I feel like I've been in a 15-round fight," he said. "I'm so drained you can't believe it."

Lost in his heroics was the fact that he'd gone three-for-four with three RBI and two runs scored.

Puckett was as good as his word: He'd gotten the Twins to the seventh game, in which anything could happen.

Puckett became a marked man the next night in Game 7. The Braves, deciding they'd take no chances, walked Puckett three times, though it mattered little as the Twins won anyway.

Photo by Richard Orndorf

It's complete jubilation as Puckett leaps into the arms of a teammate after Gene Larkin's RBI single sent Minnesota to its second world championship in four years.

Puckett continues the celebration in the madhouse that is the Metrodome.

Photo by Richard Orndorf

For nine innings in Game Seven, the Twins and Braves slammed away at each other in a scoreless tie, the first scoreless extra-inning World Series game in baseball history.

In the bottom of the 10th inning, pinch-hitter Gene Larkin put an end to it when, with the bases loaded, he hit a pop-fly over the heads of the Braves' drawn in outfield, scoring Gladden with the run that clinched the World Series.

Morris, the series MVP, was incredible. He threw 10 innings that night, allowing just seven hits and two walks while striking out eight. He refused to be pulled from the game three different times.

It was a series for the ages. Three games went to extra innings, with four decided on the final swing of the bat. It was the kind of World Series baseball needed but, unfortunately for the game, the momentum was lost two years later when a players' strike wiped out most of the second half and the entire playoffs, including the World Series.

Baseball is still trying to recover.

But for that two-week stretch, baseball had its shining moment.

"The best Series ever?" Puckett asked. "I don't know about that. But I do know it was a hell of a lot fun to play in."

Maybe that's what counts.

As it turned out, 1991 would be the pinnacle for Puckett and the Twins. Though the team played well over the next season and a half, it didn't have enough to repeat its success of '91, especially after losing Morris to free agency the following year.

But Puckett certainly did his part to try.

In 1992, Puckett got off to searing start, hitting .374 with seven homers, 25 runs batted in and an incredible .626 slugging percentage in May. He also hit his first career grand slam that month, after 5,129 at-bats and 131 career homers. For his performance, he was named American League player of the month.

Amazingly, five days after his first grand slam, he hit his second, off Toronto's Juan Guzman, and went on to be named the player of the month in June, as well, after hitting .336 with five more homers and 24 RBI. He was only the second player since the inception of the player of the month award in 1974 to earn the honor two months in a row. New York Yankee Don Mattingly had done the same in 1985.

It was a season in which he also strung together hitting streaks of 14 and 15 games.

"I was smoking early on," Puckett said.

But with that success, as well as the recent World Series title, the notoriety had become too much for Puckett, who took to using aliases when registering at hotels around the league.

For good measure, Puckett added a third grand slam in August and went on to lead the league in total bases, hits and grand slams.

He finished the year with a .329 average, 19 homers and 110 runs batted in and placed second to Oakland reliever Dennis Eckersley in the AL Most Valuable Player balloting.

In 1993, the first year of his five-year, $30 million contract, Puckett earned his eighth straight trip to the All-Star Game, this time winning the MVP award with a home run and RBI double in an AL victory.

Yet, for the first time in his career, his numbers dipped noticeably as he hit a career-worst .296 with 22 homers and 89 RBI. For most players, that's a great season. For Puckett, it was substandard.

But, perhaps more important, he was also voted baseball's best role model and the game's friendliest player in a survey by Baseball America.

But if 1993 was a down season, Puckett came back with vengeance in 1994, setting a club record with 26 RBI in April. He hit .317 with 20 homers and 112 runs batted in before the baseball strike cut the year short.

As the 1995 campaign dawned (once the strike was settled, that is), changes were in the wind for Puckett.

His playing time in center field dropped drastically and he found himself as a designated hitter more frequently, as well as playing right field and even the infield.

But it didn't affect his hitting as he posted typically solid numbers: .317 average, 23 home runs and 99 runs batted in.

But it all came to an end in the time it takes a fastball to reach home plate.

For Puckett, one catastrophic event would lead to another, though they had no connection to each other.

Look to September 28, 1995. It was a pivotal date in the history of the Minnesota Twins and of Kirby Puckett.

On that date, in a meaningless game late in a brutal Twins season, a fastball from Cleveland Indians pitcher Dennis Martinez sailed toward Puckett's face and set into motion a series of events that would change Puckett, change the Twins and change baseball forever.

This was Kirby Puckett's final at-bat in major league baseball. It came March 27, 1996 in the sixth inning of a spring training game against Atlanta. Not surprisingly, Puckett drove in a run with a single. The next morning, he awoke with blurry vision and a black dot in the middle of his right eye. He never played baseball again.

CHAPTER SIX
AN END ...
AND A BEGINNING

There was nothing he could do.

Kirby Puckett, who had always been in control of his life, his destiny, his future had faced fastballs his entire baseball life. But on this afternoon, in front of a Metrodome crowd of barely 9,000, Puckett could do nothing.

In the first inning of an eventual 12-4 Indians win over the last-place Twins, Puckett had taken his customary spot in the batter's box. Indians' starter Dennis Martinez, a close friend of Puckett's who nonetheless developed a reputation of throwing inside at hitters, did just that against Puckett.

On a 1-2 count, a fastball sailed high and tight and Puckett simply could not get out of the way.

The ball slammed into Puckett's face with a hideous crunch and he fell to the ground, a pool of blood forming next to him.

It is a baseball player's worst nightmare.

Not only is the injury potentially devastating, the emotional scars left by a beaning can be worse. Players who have never thought twice about stepping up against 90 mph heaters suddenly begin to realize how dangerous it can be. Some hitters are so intimidated and scared that they never play again.

But that was for later. At the moment, the most popular and, probably, the best player in Twins history was lying in his own blood, twisting in agony on the ground.

"It was the worst feeling I have ever had in my lifetime," Martinez said. "I almost took myself out after that inning. I understand how the fans feel. I felt just as bad, maybe worse. He's one of my best friends in baseball. We always joke around. I ask him for bats. He probably won't give me any bats anymore."

The damage was bad, but not as bad as it could have been. Puckett, who never lost consciousness, fractured his left upper jawbone, had two teeth knocked loose and suffered several cuts in his mouth.

"The left side of Kirby's nose is swollen very badly, inside and outside," said Twins team physician Dan Buss.

Surgery wasn't needed, and doctors speculated that Puckett would fully recover within four to six weeks.

In a statement the next day, Puckett exonerated Martinez of any wrongdoing.

"I know he didn't mean to hit me, his ball just moves so much," Puckett said. "Dennis is a good friend of mine and I know it wasn't intentional."

In little more than a day, Puckett received more than 200 phone calls from teammates and friends, checking up on him to see how he was doing.

For Puckett, it was a minor setback. A few weeks of rest, a little relaxing in the offseason and he'd be as good as new and ready for the 1996 season.

But it never quite worked out that way. For the first time in his baseball career, the pieces didn't fall into place. His relentless optimism was not enough. His belief that everything would work out didn't come to pass. At least not the way he expected.

His jaw healed fine and, ironically, he spoke about the beaning six months later in spring training.

"It takes more than a 90 mile-an-hour fastball to make me change," he said. "Thank God everything turned out all right, you know? It could have been much worse."

Though such an event would have changed many hitters, Puckett just took it as one more challenge. And when he stepped to the plate for his first live at-bat since being hit, he crushed a pitch 450 feet to dead center. Two innings later, he put another one out to left center.

"Everything is still the same," Puckett said. "I approach everything the same way I did before. No adjustments."

But while it appeared business as usual for Puckett, it wasn't. Nothing could have been further from the truth.

On the next morning, everything changed. That was the day Puckett awoke with a black dot in the middle of his right eye and he told his wife, Tonya, that he couldn't see her.

Assuming he'd slept on his eye wrong, Puckett didn't give that, or the blurry vision that accompanied it, much thought.

It would go away, he suspected. It had to. Besides, at age 35, he was too young to have a serious medical problem.

But the condition had been there for years, buried deep inside Kirby Puckett, a genetic chink in the armor passed down to him by his father. William Puckett had glaucoma and it was just a matter of time before his youngest son got it too.

And on the morning of March 28, when everything else seemed to be going so well, Puckett's baseball career ended. He just didn't know it.

Upon examination of Puckett's eye, doctors suspected there was a blockage of one of the veins that drained blood from the retina and the swelling was caused by the excess fluid.

Best guess? He'd be ready to play in two weeks, but it could be as long as six. But no one in late March even breathed the word retirement.

Puck retire at the peak of his skills? Never. He was indestructible. Heck, he'd never even been on the disabled list in his 11 years in the majors.

Puckett was sent to Baltimore's Johns Hopkins University Hospital to visit retinal specialist Dr. Bert Glaser. There, doctors drained fluid from the eye, gave him medication and basically told him to wait.

A few days later, Puckett was back in the Twins dugout at the Metrodome for opening day against the Detroit Tigers. But instead of manning his usual spot in the outfield, Puckett had to content himself with sitting on the bench and rooting for his teammates. It was not the easiest thing he's ever done.

"I feel great," Puckett said after the game. "Nothing hurts or anything like that."

He tapped his embattled right eye and then the left.

"This eye's got a thunderstorm and it's cloudy and this one's bright and sunny," he said. "I've just got two different shades. But it feels fine."

Puckett maintained the same furious optimism that has fueled his entire life.

"As soon as the blood starts getting to where it's supposed to go, I'll be able to see," he said. "It could happen tomorrow. It could happen next week or in two weeks or in a month. I mean, nobody knows."

But one thing Puckett did know was that his baseball career wasn't over.

Not yet. Not like this.

"He elevates a lot of people," manager Tom Kelly said. "I choose to look at things optimistically right now. Hopefully, he'll be back in a short period of time. But you don't even worry about the baseball part of things right now with Puck. When you're talking about your eyesight, the game is irrelevant. On a zero-to-10 scale, baseball is a zero."

And though his livelihood was in jeopardy, that's how Puckett approached it as well.

"I just saw a 17-year-old girl in Fort Myers who was dying of cancer," he said. "I'm 35 years old with blurred vision in one eye. Think of what happened to John McSherry today (a major league umpire who died of a heart attack during the opening day game in Cincinnati). How can I complain about anything? I'm going to live a long, fulfilling life no matter what happens."

But it was early in April that even Puckett, perhaps deep down where he didn't really want to look, began to accept that something wasn't right and that his baseball career could be over.

"My mom always told me not to worry about things I have no control over," he said.

The eye specialists in Baltimore knew only that fluid continued to build in Puckett's right eye and they didn't know why.

Puckett returned to Baltimore for more treatment and, upon his return back to Minneapolis, there was reason for optimism. Puckett's vision in his right eye, which had been only 20/200 a few days earlier, had improved to 20/100. At its worst, it had been 5/200.

"It's great that it's improved," Twins team doctor L.J. Michienzi said. "Now, it has to improve again at least that much."

Puckett admitted that he now could read a couple lines of an eye chart whereas before it was a blur. But lines on a chart are not sliders and sinkers and fastballs. No other sport relies on hand-eye coordination quite like baseball does, and without perfect vision, Puckett simply could not play.

Meanwhile, without Puckett, the Twins dugout was a strange place. Even for the opposition.

"I can't remember playing a game against the Twins and Kirby not being a part of it," said Baltimore's All-Star shortstop Cal Ripken. "It just doesn't seem right coming in here and him not being here."

The rest of the baseball world cast a worried eye toward the Twins and Puckett's future.

"I really worry about what's going on with Puck," said former teammate Pedro Munoz. "I know he can play three or four more years and no one plays the game the way he plays the game. He's been a friend to me and I'm really worried about it. I think about it all the time."

So did players around the league, many of whom couldn't conceive of baseball without Puckett.

But the ailment continued to baffle doctors, and though many had opinions of what could be afflicting the Twins superstar, no one could pinpoint it exactly.

For Puckett the days dragged on.

"When I wake up every morning, I open my right eye first," he said. "I want to see right away if I can see clearly. I hope every night that I'll be able to see the next morning."

But every morning, nothing had changed. And even the optimistic Puckett was beginning to show hints of frustration.

"The doctors keep telling me that they can't find anything wrong with me," he said. "I keep passing all the tests. So I guess they're going to keep looking. The doc keeps telling me he can't find anything to work with. I hope we see something soon. There's no timetable. There's nothing I can do but wait."

In the meantime, Puckett hung out in the clubhouse and the dugout, dressing in his Twins uniform every game (at least when he wasn't in Baltimore for more tests) and doing his part to help his team. Other times, he'd take his bat, look in a mirror and practice a swing he wasn't sure he'd ever get to use again.

"I'm handling this a lot better than I thought I would," he said. "I thought I'd be going crazy, but I'm OK. But I can't sit still that long."

Finally, on April 13, after days of uncertainty, Glaser announced the results of an exhaustive battery of tests.

Puckett was in the early stages of glaucoma, an affliction in which excessive fluid builds up inside the eye and causes extreme pressure. In many cases, glaucoma can cause blindness, but Glaser said he was optimistic Puckett would be able to play baseball again in 1996.

"I believe we'll see an improvement but it's too early to predict any outcome," Glaser said.

Said Puckett: "I've got the best doctor there is. All I can do is pray. I can still see my beautiful wife and kids. Even if I can't play anymore, all I can do is be thankful."

What followed a few days later was an experimental laser surgery in which Glaser opened several small holes in the back of Puckett's eye to help fluid drain.

It worked well enough that by early May, Puckett was told he'd have a 50-50 chance of regaining full vision.

But by that point, Puckett had grown increasingly frustrated by the lack of progress and even considered taking live batting practice.

"Watch me," he said prior to the start of a series in Anaheim, the place where he made his major league debut 12 years earlier. "I'll be out there. All eyes will be on me. Maybe."

And though Puckett was joking, it was clear the months of inactivity were starting to wear on him.

"I'm tired of shagging for other guys," he said. "I haven't hit anything moving since March 27."

Finally, on May 11, Puckett got his wish and stepped back in the batting cage to take a few cuts against the 50 mile-an-hour fastballs of Twins coach Ron Gardenhire.

He sent three balls out of the park, an impressive display for a guy who was essentially hitting with one eye.

"I still can't hit," Puckett said afterward. "I wish I could hit with one eye but I can't. If someone threw me a curveball, I wouldn't have a chance."

Over the course of the next two weeks, Puckett made another trip to Baltimore then made two trips to the prestigious Mayo Clinic in Rochester, Minn. for a second opinion. In that time, Puckett was either improving, staying the same or getting worse, depending on what you read and who you believed. Different experts said Puckett would return in two weeks to play or a month or maybe later during the season.

In short, after two months, nobody knew.

"He can do everything but play," a frustrated Michienzi said.

A second laser surgery was performed June 7, followed by a third on June 18. But nothing changed.

Finally, in what was seen as an almost last-ditch effort, Glaser performed a surgical procedure called a vitrectomy on July 12. That surgery called for three incisions in Puckett's right eye, in which Glaser inserted three needles. The first would remove the blood from near the retina. The second would inject saline solution to replace the blood and the third needle would have light shined through it to help Glaser operate.

The hope, slim as it was, was that by removing the excess blood, the blurry vision would at least clear up and the process of healing the retina could begin.

But the surgery only confirmed what Glaser had suspected, and what Twins fans and all of baseball had dreaded.

"I knew that it wasn't going to get any better," said Glaser. "The retina will not recover."

That was that.

Kirby Puckett's right eye, which had been fine on the evening of March 27 in preparation for a new season, was useless.

Ironically, the beaning Puckett had suffered late the previous season in no way impacted what happened later.

Puckett was done with baseball. But baseball was far from done with him.

"I was prepared," Puckett said. "I mean, there's no way you can be prepared for this, but I was prepared for life after baseball. I was just happy. It was a relief for me to have it off my shoulders. Even though I knew the news was bad for myself and the Twins and the people involved with baseball in the Twin Cities, I was happy just to know."

On July 12, Puckett, in front of a packed, sobbing room inside the Metrodome, made a clean break with the game he had given so much to and which had rewarded him back so many times.

Twins' public relations director Sean Harlin remembered the scene.

"First of all, it was the biggest press conference ever held in this state," he said. "It was sad. I was in the front and I introduced everybody. And to look out at the audience and see more media than I'd ever seen before, it was amazing. And it was the most somber, sad faces I'd ever see.

"Everyone was crying. Everyone except for Kirby. It was like he was making everyone else OK. I wasn't surprised with the way he handled it. I was amazed, but I wasn't surprised. He's like a rock."

Here is the text of Puckett's news conference. It speaks for itself.

The indelible images of Kirby Puckett's retirement announcement on July 12, 1996. "Everyone knew it was bad," said Twins director of communications Dave St. Peter. "But we never knew it was this bad."

Well, I think that I could tell when Kent Hrbek was sitting in front — the last time I was in here, he was doing this and Herbie said that this wasn't an easy room. And he was right.

But for me, a kid growing up in Chicago, coming out of a bad neighborhood, people never thought that I would do anything. And here I am sitting in front of you guys, and the only sad thing, the only thing I regret that I have about this game at all is that I know I could have done so much better if I could've played.

But then again, that is 20/20, something else could have happened. I mean, who knows? But I think that anybody who knows me, including my teammates, know that every time I put that uniform on, that I laugh and joke with the opposition. But when it was time to get it on, I got it on and I gave it everything I had. And that is what I try and tell the young guys here, is to enjoy life. I mean every day. You don't get four hits every day — well, maybe Knobby (second baseman Chuck Knoblauch) ... maybe Molly (Paul Molitor) — but just because you don't get a hit doesn't mean you don't make a good defensive play, or run the bases good, or do whatever.

At this time, I have so many people to thank. First of all, I would like to thank my beautiful wife for putting up with me for 11 years now.

And the world is not over now guys ... I can't see out of my right eye, but I am still as healthy as ever. I want to go on with my life. I have saved my money good, I mean my agent is right here, you know. Carl (Pohlad, the Twins' owner) is right here, the boys are here, everybody is here ... including T.K. (manager Tom Kelly), who's had to put up with me for 15 or so years. And Aggie (Rick Aguilera), and Molly, all my teammates present, you guys (the media), I love all of you guys. And I want you guys to go out there tonight and you know what you've got to do. If you don't win, I don't want to talk to you no more.

This is kind of a day that I was really ... that I've been really not looking forward to doing, but some things happen and there is no reason for them. Like I talked to my wife at night sometimes, I talk to Ron and Mike and I say "You know what, somebody gave me this for a reason, and sometimes there are no reasons for things that happen, they just happen." And you guys know how I am. I am a pretty upbeat person all the time, and I come to the ballpark and I play.

As I look around this room with my good eye, with the 20/20 vision that I do have, I see my good buddy Dennis Martinez sitting in the back and he took a lot of crap for the accident that happened last year. And I am here to tell you that I love Dennis and he didn't try to do that on purpose ... I was leaning out there, I was cheating a little bit and I got caught out there naked. And I couldn't get out of the way. I mean, it wasn't his fault. It was me. Knobby was on third base, the infield was back and I was trying to drive in my 100th run. I was trying to do that. That's my job.

And I want to tell my teammates that you're not getting rid of me. I will be around. Maybe not as much...but I will be around because I love you guys, and you guys know how I feel about this game.

I would like to thank Carl Pohlad and Jerry Bell and everybody for giving me the opportunity to wear this uniform that I have on, just like Kent Hrbek, only one uniform. And I am proud to say that I am a Minnesota Twin. You know how some people say they bleed the Yankee pinstripes and Dodger blue? Well, whatever you want to call this, I wore one uniform in my career and I am proud to say that.

On my hat, I have No. 29 ... That was for Rod Carew, whose daughter passed away. Anytime you guys sit around and think I have it bad, I know these cameras are shining on me and I want to tell that I love you so much too, but Rod had an unfortuancy in his life, also. He lost his little baby girl and I have two little kids at home, they're still healthy, my wife is healthy, I'm healthy, in shape — somewhat. Like Herbie said, I don't have to get in shape no more, right Herbie? And I am looking forward to that, but I am going to try and stay in shape somewhat.

I love the game, and I thought I played the game with a certain amount of pride and respect every time. I know I didn't get hits every time. I know that I got geezed a lot and I laugh at Molly and I do my fellow thing and I watch Knobby and these guys play. Even the pitchers. I've been talking to pitchers — I don't know how to pitch. (Scott) Aldred will tell you, he came over from Detroit and I said, "Dred, man, just throw strikes, just believe in yourself." I don't know what to tell him. I am not a pitcher. But he is doing a lot better than he was, where he was. Marty Cordova used my bats every day. Rookie of the year, used my bats last year. Did I get anything from Marty? No. But he always says it is coming, whatever that means.

It is a tough day for me, because, and I can't sit and lie to you and say to you that I am not going to miss the game, because I am. I have missed it since March 28, when I haven't been able to perform. But, I have still come to the ballpark. I've messed around with Stelly (coach Rick Stelmazek) and Scotty Ullger and Gardy (coach, Ron Gardenhire) and Bert Blyleven, the announcer. Now Bert, your job is in jeopardy, babe. I am coming after you.

Dick Bremer, all you guys, I told you I was coming to get you.

It has been nice for me. I've been a Minnesota Twin, this is my 13th year, and I am proud to say that I have played with a lot of pride, a lot of class and integrity when I put the uniform on, and that is the part that I miss the most. The camaraderie with my teammates, and starting up trouble. My wife is really going to get mad. I can't start up any trouble at home because my kids are against me. But it is going to be all right. I am going to miss T.K., I am going to miss all of you guys, but I am not going anywhere. I will be here, but I just won't be putting this on anymore. This is the last time that you will see Kirby Puckett in a Minnesota Twins uniform.

And I just want to tell you all that I love you all so much. Paul Molitor came over this year and I was looking so forward to playing with Molly this year. And in spring training, we had Knobby, Molly and myself and we were doing so good and I was so excited. I was hitting about .360 in spring training. I was looking so forward to talking to Molly and Knobby and it is incredible to see the start that they have gotten off to and how many RBIs I would have by now. I guess that's pretty selfish ... but that's my job.

And I want to tell all you press people thank you very much for being behind me and putting all of those good things in about me and all those bad things about me, too. But I don't mind the criticism because if you can't take the heat then get out of the kitchen. And I am here to tell you that I stay in the kitchen all of the time because I know how to handle it. I am not afraid to fail, and I have always thrown myself out there no matter what.

Just like I did in Game Six, when we were struggling and I told you guys to jump on, we jumped on and we went. But I have never been afraid to fail. It is kind of like Ozzie Smith said, it is time for another part, not a new part, but a great part of my life. Ever since I was five years old — I am 35 years old — sitting in front of you now and I have played baseball ever since then for 30 years and it's been a great part of my life. It really has.

But now it is time for me to close the chapter in this book on baseball and go on to another part of my life. It is going to be all right. Kirby Puckett is going to be all right. Don't worry about me. I will show up, but I am going to have fun and have a smile on my face. The only thing is that I won't have this uniform on. But you guys have a lot of memories of what I did when I did have it on.

And I am going to tell my young teammates to know right now, that when you put that uniform on, you put it on and you play with pride and integrity, the way Kent Hrbek plays with it, played with it. And Paul Molitor and Knobby, and all of you guys play with it. Just don't take it for granted because you never know, tomorrow is not promised to any of us. Anything can happen to any of us, whether we're reporters or whatever we may be — anything can happen.

So enjoy yourself. I love you all. Thank you very much.

The speech was not prepared. Puckett said he spoke simply from the heart.

"Kirby was never known as a great wordsmith," said Twins director of communications Dave St. Peter. "But he gave one of the more eloquent speeches ever given by a baseball player. He was able to put it all in perspective. He wanted everyone to know he didn't die that day, he just isn't playing baseball anymore."

His departure from baseball hit the Twins, the state of Minnesota and baseball in general like a thunderbolt.

It especially clobbered Twins players, many of whom were youngsters and had grown up watching and idolizing Puckett.

In fact, when manager Tom Kelly called a team meeting to announce Puckett's decision and that there would be a press conference to make it official, some of the younger players didn't know if they should go.

"Then they passed word around that we are all going to go together," said utility player Denny Hocking. "They said it would be better if the whole team went together. It was really sad."

Puckett, in fact, insisted on it.

"I wanted my younger teammates to know how lucky they are," he said.

Even a veteran like Paul Molitor, who had just joined his hometown team that season after successful stints in Milwaukee and Toronto, was shaken.

"I was pretty much taken aback by the completeness of the (test) results found," he said. "The idea in here was that Kirby wasn't going to play this year, but people were holding onto optimism that somehow, some way, this thing was going to turn around."

Soon after, Molitor and the other Twins listened in tears as Puckett stepped away.

"I might have lost a teammate, but I sure haven't lost a good friend," Molitor said.

Former Twin and teammate Kent Hrbek recalled when he was a kid what it was like when his idol, Harmon Killebrew, retired.

"I thought that was the end of the world," he said. "People are going to miss Kirby, but people have to realize that Kirby is not going to play until he's 90."

It was especially hard on Puckett's favorite manager, Tom Kelly.

Kelly had watched Puckett from the time he was a raw kid in rookie ball at Elizabethton, Tenn., and he had seen something special then.

Over the years, Kelly and Puckett had grown and evolved together. Together, they had seen the bad times and the good.

"It was a pleasure for me and every other Twins' fan, and baseball fan, to be able to sit and watch every game he played," Kelly said. "How lucky am I? Thanks."

There was also an outpouring and love and respect and sadness from the rest of baseball as well.

"This is sad day for the game of baseball," said Baltimore Orioles coach Elrod Hendricks, who respected Puckett so much he wore Puckett's No. 34 on his cap in hopes he'd recover.

"The game only needs another 600 Kirby Pucketts," he continued. "He's meant so much to the game — not only in the way he played, but in the warmth he always had for everyone."

There were many others as well.

"He was certainly one guy who I'll always remember having a real enthusiasm for the game," said veteran Detroit Tigers infielder Alan Trammel. "I know that can be overused, but I don't think there's one player who doesn't like him."

"He had that happy spirit and enthusiasm he brought to the park every day," said another Tiger, Cecil Fielder. "It's not good; to lose a champion like that is not good."

"He was one of those players that other players look up to, that other players would pay to see," said Boston Red Sox infielder Tim Naehring.

Former teammate Chili Davis was shaken by the news too.

"There are only three or four guys I've met in baseball who if they asked me to do anything, I would, and he's one of them," Davis said. "He's a special human being. I wish I could say the same about myself."

Milwaukee Brewers manager Phil Garner was in his office prior to his team's game when word came down that Puckett had retired. Garner lit a cigar and shook his head sadly.

"This is a big loss for baseball," he said. "A big loss."

Few people argued.

Some hoped it was a cruel hoax.

Photo by Richard Orndorf

Kirby Puckett makes his way down the Metrodome steps prior to the start of the celebration in his honor.

"He can't retire," said Orioles' first baseman Rafael Palmeiro. "Maybe he can just take the rest of the year off and come back. He's better with one eye than most guys are with two. I have to give him a call. I have to talk to him. It's just not baseball without him."

The outpouring of emotion took Puckett by surprise.

"I didn't think it was possible to be more popular out of the game than I was in it," he said. "That amazes me. The response from everybody has been awesome."

It is March 1997, and Puckett is back at the Twins spring training complex in Fort Myers, Fla.

He is completely blind in his right eye.

"Midnight," he said. "Zero."

He now holds a title in the Twins front office though Puckett makes fun of it, as he does with everything else.

"I'm the executive vice president in charge of A to Z," he said. "I'm the executive vice president slash, slash, slash. If you want to reach me it's slash dot com on the Internet. Not that I know anything about computers. But it must be an important title. The last one to hold it here was Andy McPhail."

This is life for Kirby Puckett now.

He sits in his office in Florida and signs thousands of autographs. And once the season starts, he'll be back in the Twin Cities, rooting on his team and doing whatever he can to make people's lives a little easier, a little more fun. He still plans to buy that fishing boat he's always wanted but there is always time for that.

He'd like to own part of the Twins. He'd like to see his team get a new baseball-only stadium. And if he can be the voice to get that accomplished, he will gladly do it.

"There's a great sense of community pride with Kirby Puckett," St. Peter said. "He's our Michael Jordan, our Larry Bird."

And the hope is that Puckett will somehow find a way to take the way he played baseball and transfer it to the youngsters playing the game now, the ones who play the game but don't respect it.

"The game misses Kirby Puckett," said Boston Red Sox first baseman Mo Vaughn. "It misses a player who exemplifies the way the game should be played. It misses his personality. It misses his attitude. He is somebody young people ought to study."

In the year 2001, Kirby Puckett will be eligible for induction into the Baseball Hall of Fame. And already the question is being asked: Does he belong?

Puckett has heard it before and will hear it again until his bust finds its place in Cooperstown. N.Y. But his answer is always the same.

"It's not up to me," he said. "It's out of my control, so I don't worry about it. It was my job to play and I did that. Now it's up to the people who vote."

But NBC broadcaster and close friend Bob Costas sees Puckett as a cinch to reach the Hall.

"I think he'll go in on the first ballot," he said. "What he accomplished, with those two World Series, if he'd been unremarkable as a person, he would still get in. But there certainly won't be anyone who will withhold a vote because of a grudge against Kirby. I

Kirby Puckett speaks to a sellout crowd as he introduces a video honoring his life and career with the Twins that was unveiled in the fall of 1996. The video was narrated by his longtime friend Bob Costas.

Two generations of baseball greatness meet during Kirby Puckett Night in September of 1996. Here, former Twins great (and then a coach for the California Angels) Rod Carew congratulates Puckett on his career. Carew and Puckett may well be the two most synonymous names ever with the Twins.

don't know of anyone who has one. I don't think there's much doubt he should be there."

The Minneapolis Star-Tribune did an informal poll of 35 baseball writers who vote on Hall of Fame inductees. Of those, 23 said they would definitely vote for Puckett and most said they'd vote for him on the first ballot. Nine others said they were undecided, though five of them leaned toward voting for him.

That's a powerful endorsement for a player without any of the traditional big numbers that insure enshrinement.

He ended his career with 2,304 hits, though if he'd played the three or four more years he envisioned, he likely would have reached that magical 3,000-hit plateau.

He hit 207 career home runs, drove in 1,085 runs, scored 1,071 runs, had a career batting average of .318, won six Gold Gloves and was named to 10 straight All-Star teams.

But Kirby Puckett was never about the numbers. He was about the joy and the love and the fun of baseball. He was the reason why 8-year-old kids pick up a baseball glove in the first place. He played hard because to do less would have been an insult to the game.

What he brought to baseball, and what he leaves baseball, is the feeling that anything is possible.

Perhaps Costas summed it up best.

"My reaction (when Puckett retired) was that it's a shame that he's been cheated out of how many years he had left," he said.

"But it was more than that. I felt it was especially bad for baseball, when there are so few people in the game you can feel good about without reservation, Kirby was one of them. There are certain players that, every time you see them, you can remind yourself why you like the game.

"It's a shame the game was deprived of his presence on the field. I thought of all the kids who liked to watch him play and how they'd miss him. He handled his circumstances with grace and without bitterness. A lot of times in sports now, we're so cynical that we all try to look for the dark side and that if an athlete has a good image, it must be that — an image. But this guy refused to do that. He's just a genuinely good person."

Photo by Richard Orndorf

He belongs in a baseball cap and spikes, not a shirt and tie. But that is the best Kirby Puckett can do now with a right eye that's completely blind. He will continue to work for the Twins and is a major force in trying to get a new baseball-only stadium built for the team. "I'll always be a Twin," he said.

CHAPTER SEVEN
LIFE AFTER PUCK

I t's not a pretty sight, this life after Puck.

We look at baseball and we see grim desolation, we see uncertainty, we see a game going nowhere fast and in a big hurry to get there.

We see players who not only don't respect the game they've been lucky enough to star in, but don't even seem to like the game all that much.

We see a game that has lost its way.

For many reasons — from a bitter labor struggle to skyrocketing salaries to the influx and growth of other sports — baseball has been left behind.

Quaint, anachronistic baseball — the game our parents and

Photo by Richard Orndorf

Though retired, Puckett remains active in the Twins organization, though he jokingly says he's vice president of nothing in particular. His presence alone means a lot to the Twins and their fans.

grandparents loved — is no longer America's favorite pastime and, if the truth be known, has not been for years.

But there was something about baseball that kept tugging at us, like some puppy pulling at a pants leg. Come back, it would say. Come back, and we'll show you just how important the game should be, must be, to America.

But somewhere along the line, all of that stopped working. Baseball lost its way and Americans dutifully followed.

Now the game that defined America is trying to battle its way back into the consciousness of a country. And baseball seemed to be winning the battle, or at least had stopped the rampant defections and disinterest that had hallmarked the sport for too many years.

The 1996 baseball season would be the one where baseball got its fans back. The disastrous and painful work stoppage was two years in the past. New ideas, like wild-card playoffs and inter-league play, were being instituted. And though such changes made the purists howl, it was at least a step in the right direction.

Baseball's powers that be seemed to have finally awakened to the realization that more was needed to sell their game than grainy black and white film of Joe DiMaggio and Babe Ruth. Baseball needed an ambassador, a player who could show what made this game special, so special that it enraptured a nation for decades.

That player, it appeared, was Kirby Puckett.

And why not?

Here was a guy who was the embodiment of the American dream. He was no physical specimen at 5-foot-8 and 200 pounds (depending on what scale you used, that is). He readily, even gleefully,

admitted that he was no Rhodes scholar and had no desire to be
one.

Kirby Puckett was a baseball player. From start to finish. Nothing
more, nothing less. He began playing the game at age 5, darting
among the concrete canyons of Chicago's Robert Taylor Homes,
one of the most dangerous strips of real estate in America.

But that didn't matter to Puckett, who played the game from
sunup to sundown, pushed relentlessly by the belief that he would
someday make it to the big leagues.

Isn't that every kid's fondest fantasy? To play pro baseball. To hit
the winning home run. To strike out that slugger with the bases
loaded in the seventh game of the World Series. To play a kid's
game as a adult. What could be better?

For Puckett, absolutely nothing. Which made him baseball's perfect ambassador. He demanded nothing from baseball except the
chance to prove himself. When baseball gave him that chance, he
took care of the rest. Is there anything more American than that?

For 12 years, Kirby Puckett did for baseball what no one else in
the game could do. He played it with a raw abandon. He played it
with a youthful exuberance, as though nothing else mattered in
the world.

In short, he played the game the way it was meant to be played.
And along the way, he brought a legion of fans with him.

Remember, Kirby Puckett played in a relative baseball wasteland
in Minnesota. In fact, when the Twins roared almost out of
nowhere to win the World Series in 1987, it was considered little
more than a fluke.

But while the Twins were an unknown quantity, Puckett was already a name. In fact, he may have been the only Twin most baseball fans outside the state of Minnesota could name.

That is what Kirby Puckett brought to baseball. A recognition and a feeling that if Puckett could do it, anyone could.

Yes he had the skills. But it was more than that. He proved that you could be a perennial All-Star and still be a human being. He proved you could win two World Series titles and still say hi to people walking down the street. He proved you could make $6 million a season and treat the less fortunate with the dignity and kindness they deserve.

For Kirby Puckett, there was no other way to live.

That's why his retirement in July of 1996 was so stunning, so sad, so unfair.

He was a guy who had never been injured a day in his career. Yet one morning during spring training, he awoke to find a black dot in the middle of his eye. Literally overnight, his life was turned upside down. Four months later, Puckett was forced to give up the game he loves because of the onset of glaucoma.

Just like that, the best thing baseball had going for it is gone.

No, maybe it's not fair and maybe, in the short run, baseball will suffer more. But just maybe this is some strange blessing in disguise for the game.

Puckett? Heck, he'll be fine. Guys like him always are. Optimistic and happy and simply glad to be alive, Kirby Puckett will flourish no matter what he does.

For years Puckett was known for keeping the Twins bench loose with his chatter and relentless optimism.

But for the game, this may have been, in some weird way, exactly what it needed. This forces baseball to find a new Kirby Puckett, a new force, a new player who exudes joy and fun. Maybe this is baseball's chance to find Puckett's heir apparent. And if anyone wants the job, they certainly have the blueprint for it.

But it will not be an easy role to fill. In fact, it may be impossible. You don't duplicate a Kirby Puckett, you only hope to find enough to allow yourself into the same ballpark with him.

"What can you say about Kirby," said one of baseball's great sphinxes, Eddie Murray, who was about as far on the other side of the spectrum from Puckett as anyone could be. "He is what baseball is all about. He will be missed."

Puckett has even admitted his amazement to the response his retirement has triggered. He knew he was a popular among players, certainly among Twins fans and surely with baseball fans in general. But the outpouring of emotion, sadness, even grief after his announcement knocked him off-stride.

"I'm just a baseball player," he has said.

But to a generation of baseball fans who had few other stars to turn to, Puckett was something special. Upon hearing of his retirement, kids at a local junior high expressed their sadness.

"This is bad," said one 14-year-old boy. "Everybody loves him. They like him because he plays because he loves to play. He doesn't do it just for the money. He puts his heart into the game. And he's not snotty like the other players."

For some reason, it always seems to come back to that regarding Kirby Puckett.

Some of the images that will stay with Twins fans, and baseball fans in general, about Kirby Puckett, baseball's last warrior.

Photo by Richard Orndorf

Photo by Richard Orndorf

He's not like the other players.

He has never been like the other players. He was only being himself.

"Kirby knows fans and he knows his community, and that's what makes baseball tick," said another fan. "I do love baseball and Kirby keeps the interest in baseball here. They went to games to pay him respect."

Still another fan: "If half the bums in this game had half his class, it would be a great game."

What Kirby Puckett did during his career was show baseball how good it was and how good it could be again. He also showed that it really wasn't that difficult to accomplish.

As a result, fair or not, Puckett has been hung with the label of hero. It is a word that is thrown around far too casually these days and, because it has, it has lost its very meaning.

Kirby Puckett would be the first to argue that he's no hero. Someone who runs into a burning building to save three children is a hero. Someone who dives into a raging river to save another from drowning is a hero. Puckett would cackle at the thought of being placed in that category.

All Kirby has ever done, and ever wanted to do, was play baseball. And from 1984 until his untimely exit in 1996, there were few who did it better.

So now baseball must trudge on without him.

Former Twins teammate Randy Bush reflected on his good friend.

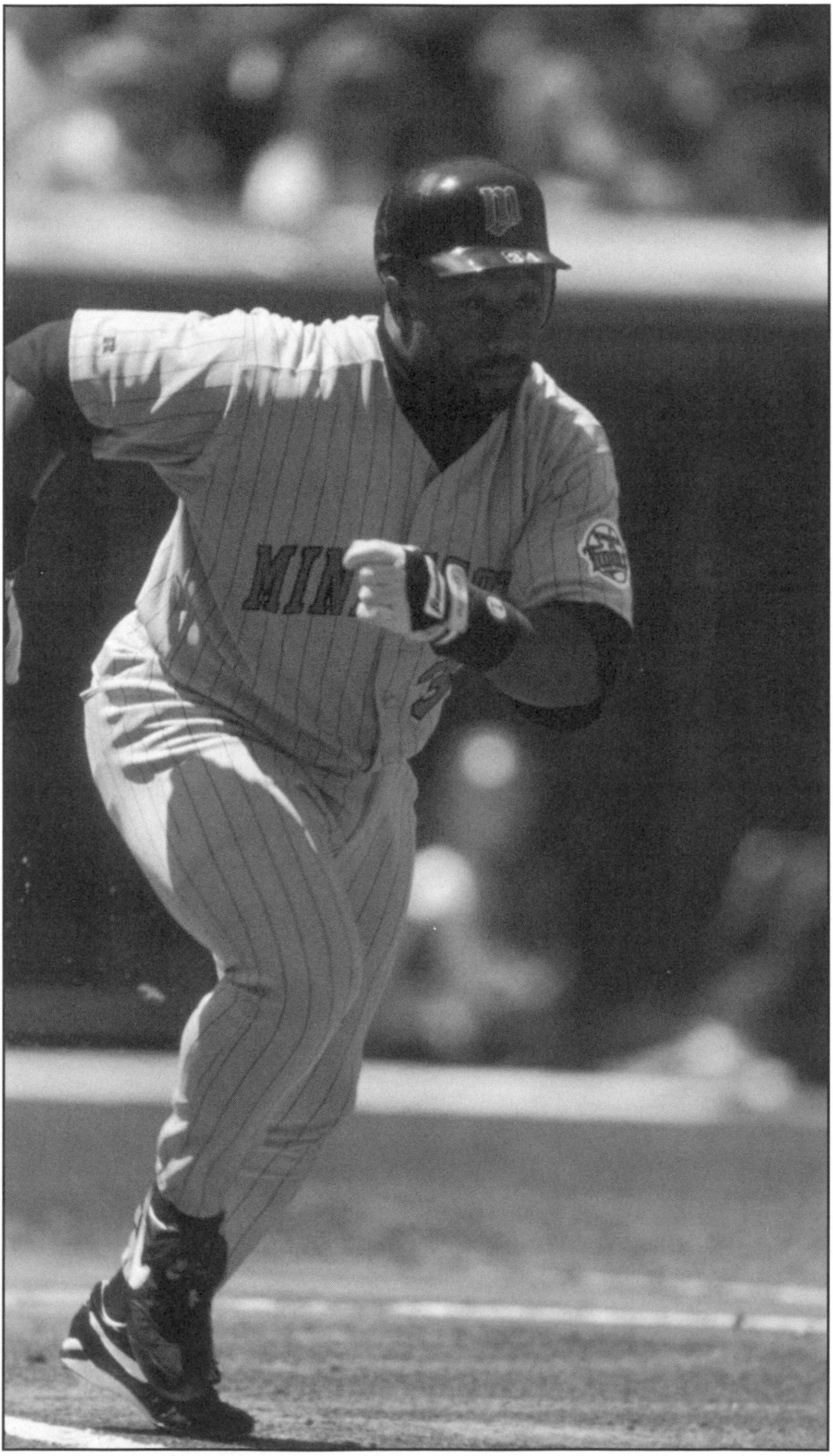

Photo by Richard Orndorf

"I was sad when I heard (of his retirement)," he said. "And it also made me feel old. As long as Puck was out there, I could say, 'I'm not old. I'd still be playing if I had enough ability.' Now I know the truth. I'm old."

But Bush turned serious.

"This is not the way it should end for Kirby Puckett," he said. "He's a wonderful person — always upbeat and positive, and he would have been the same if he was running a carwash. I guess that's what he's going to do now. Buy that carwash he was always talking about."

And the funny thing is, he probably would be happy doing it.

In a poignant twist, Puckett found himself talking with a Twin Cities newspaper reporter early during his star-crossed 1996 spring training. This was before he awoke with a damaged eye. This was before the months of uncertainty. This was before his neat, order-ly, perfect world collapsed.

"People say, 'You're so lucky, you have so much money,' " he told the writer. "That's not everything to me. I'm not extravagant. Give me my blue jeans and my truck. That's all I need to get around."

After a pause, Puckett turned unusually reflective.

"You never know," he said. "What you have today can be gone tomorrow. There are no guarantees in life."

Four months later, he was proven eerily, sadly, correct.

But Puckett has no regrets. That's another trademark of this man. Like some oversized rubber ball, he can take the worst licking and continue to bound back, as good as before. Nothing stops him.

Nothing even slows him down. There is too much to do, too much to enjoy. Sure, a baseball career may be over, but that only means a new door is opening for something else.

With some people, such an attitude would seem cloying and fake. With Puckett, it seems perfectly natural, perfectly Puckett.

So, what will life after Puck be like? How will baseball deal with yet another blow it cannot afford to sustain? Where will the game go from here? And, more important, who will take it where it needs to go?

None of these questions have easy answers. But just consider where baseball was when Puckett made his debut in 1984.

The charismatic Reggie Jackson was in the twilight of his career, as was Pete Rose and several other superstars. They were baseball's goodwill ambassadors then.

At the same time, a new crop of young stars were coming up. Players like Cal Ripken, Paul Molitor and Don Mattingly were just hitting their stride while Robin Yount, George Brett and Eddie Murray were reaching the pinnacles of their career.

When Puckett came to the big leagues, baseball was still enjoying a golden time. It didn't need overt displays of affection because America, and Americans, still loved baseball.

Over the years, while those attitudes changed, Puckett did not. He remained true to baseball's nature.

It is for that reason, and maybe that reason alone, that there is hope for the game. Kirby Puckett has shown to everyone that baseball has been, should be and always will be a game, no matter what others try to do.

Photo by Richard Orndorf

Puckett will be eligible for Hall of Fame induction in 2001, many believe he will be elected on the first ballot

"It seems like whenever (bad) things happen you hear a lot of players say it's a chance to be reminded of your priorities," Molitor said. "But it shouldn't take those things to remind us. When we're playing a game, we should have fun and do our best. It shouldn't take somebody being removed to realize just what a great opportunity we have."

If that's the legacy Kirby Puckett leaves, it's fine with him. If the premature way he left the game he loved has an impact in other players, his job is complete.

Puckett never set out to change baseball. He never set out to be a pioneer. He only wanted a chance to play the game he knew he could excel at. He wanted to enjoy playing baseball and he wanted those who watched him to enjoy it, too.

That's not a lot to ask.

And if today's players can learn that simple truism, then there may indeed be life after Puck.

Photo by Richard Orndorf